P9-CQM-520

Children's Literature in the Reading Program

Bernice E. Cullinan, Editor
New York University

ON LOAN FROM
THE READING CENTRE

READING CENTRE LIBRARY

The conditions for borrowing books are as follows:

1. Books are on loan for a three week period.

2. A telephone request may be made to have the borrowing period extended for another three weeks ONLY. **Phone 439-8292.**

3. Books must be **returned promptly** to the library, either in person or via board courier service to **The Reading Centre, c/o G.B. Little Jr. P.S.**

4. It is expected that **LOST BOOKS** will be **REPLACED** by the borrower.

ira

Published by the
International Reading Association
Newark, Delaware 19714

INTERNATIONAL READING ASSOCIATION

OFFICERS
1986-1987

President   Roselmina Indrisano, Boston University, Boston, Massachusetts

Vice President   Phylliss J. Adams, University of Denver, Denver, Colorado

Vice President Elect   Patricia S. Koppman, PSK Associates, San Diego, California

Executive Director   Ronald W. Mitchell, International Reading Association, Newark, Delaware

DIRECTORS

Term Expiring Spring 1987
    Carl Braun, University of Calgary, Calgary, Alberta, Canada
    Nora Forester, Northside Independent School District, San Antonio, Texas
    Susan Mandel Glazer, Rider College, Lawrenceville, New Jersey

Term Expiring Spring 1988
    Margaret Pope Hartley, The Psychological Corporation, North Little Rock, Arkansas
    P. David Pearson, University of Illinois, Champaign, Illinois
    Carol M. Santa, School District #5, Kalispell, Montana

Term Expiring Spring 1989
    Marie C. DiBiasio, Bristol Public Schools, Bristol, Rhode Island
    Hans U. Grundin, The Open University, Milton Keynes, England
    Nancy E. Seminoff, Winona State University, Winona, Minnesota

Copyright 1987 by the
International Reading Association, Inc.

Library of Congress Cataloging-in-Publication Data

Children's literature in the reading program.

    Includes bibliographies and index.
    1. Reading (Elementary)–United States. 2. Children's
literature–United States.   3. English language–Study
and teaching (Elementary)–United States.   I. Cullinan,
Bernice E.
LB1573.C455   1987   372.4   86-27786
ISBN O-87207-782-9
Third Printing October 1987

Contents

ON LOAN FROM
THE READING CENTRE

Graphic design by Larry Husfelt

Cover art by Tomie dePaola

Foreword

The day I had been waiting for for a year and a half had arrived.

I was finally old enough to go to school. I was so happy and insisted on walking the last block by myself and going alone into the school building. All around me were crying children clinging to their mothers (little did I know that I would share classrooms with these same children for thirteen years!), but not me! I went directly to the lady standing there (who I found out shortly was the principal) and asked where the kindergarten room was, please. Poor Miss Imick, the kindergarten teacher. After introducing myself to her, I immediately confronted her with "When do we learn how to *READ*?" "Oh," she replied, "we don't learn how to read in kindergarten, we learn how to read next year." "All right," I announced, "I'll be back next year." and promptly walked out the forbidden front door and trudged all the way home. The school telephoned my mother. The police were called, my father rushed home from the barbershop where he worked. I was calmly sitting up in the attic "reading" one of my mother's slightly racy novels–upside down.

You see, it was of the utmost importance for me to learn to read for many reasons. One being that as far back as I could remember, my mother read aloud to my older brother and me and I just knew that all kinds of wonderful stories and interesting things were there for the taking between the covers of books. What I didn't like, however, was always being at the mercy of my mother's timetable for the daily read aloud session. I wanted to find out all this stuff when *I* wanted to find it out.

Second, in my hometown, the children's librarian (pronounced *liberrian*) at the public library (pronounced *liberry*) insisted that before a library card was issued to any child, a form must be signed by the classroom teacher stating that the child could indeed read. Don't ask me the logic behind this except that perhaps she felt that children who didn't know how to read didn't *deserve* books or they would "break" them.

My mother and father knew that threats of punishment wouldn't budge me from my resolve not to get back to school until the "next year" when I would learn to read, so the logical approach was used. "You know," my mother said, "if you don't *pass* kindergarten you can't go into first grade." So, reluctantly I went to kindergarten where we "played," which was a waste of time as far as I was concerned.

Obviously, the first grade teacher, Miss Kiniry, knew all about me by the time the following September came because when I confronted her with, "Are we really going to learn to read this year?" she answered "Yes–on Friday–in the afternoon."

I figured I could wait the two and a half days and sure enough when we entered the classroom, on the table in the front of the room were three piles of books, one red, one blue, and one yellow. The red ones were bright and shining new, the blue ones were in fairly good condition but certainly not new, and the yellow ones looked as though they had been dragged behind a truck. Miss Kiniry told us that they were all the same inside, but the different colors were for the three different reading groups. Instinctively, we all knew that if you were given a new red book it meant you were in the best reading group and so on down through the other colors. The yellow group was obviously going to be the slow readers. It all connected somehow (we weren't sure how) to the elusive library card. Slow readers get battered books, fast readers get new ones.

I did the only thing I knew to do in crisis situations. I began to pray and, miracle of miracles, I was given a RED book.

"Now class," said Miss Kiniry, "leave your books on the desk and don't open them until I tell you." Of course, I opened mine very quickly to sneak a peek, and to my complete disappointment I was confronted with Dick and Jane and Spot and Puff. To this day I remember the sinking feeling in my stomach when I saw those sanitized illustrations of those BORING PEOPLE. The sinking feeling only got worse when Miss Kiniry began with "See Dick run. Run, Dick, run. Run, run, run. See Dick run."

NOBODY, nobody talked like that, at least not in my life. This was not my idea of what books and learning to read were all about. I was in deep trouble. It was even more imperative that I get my library card, so I could get REAL books. So, I did the forbidden thing. I took my reading book home, shoved up under my sweater. My mother quietly called Miss Kiniry to tell her. "I know," she said, "I saw him leave the room with a very flat stomach. But, it's all right. He has such an urgency to learn to read." My mother explained why.

All weekend I walked around with that awful textbook and asked my mother and father "What's this word? What's this one?" By Monday morning, I had "learned" to read and promptly informed Miss Kiniry of that fact. She suffered through my reading the entire reader to her–"Run, run, run. Look, look, look, etc." and graciously signed the form from the library. Life was certainly looking up. I could get my library card–I could get my hands on *real* books. But that's another story.

This all does say something to me, though. We often underestimate children. If I knew that Dick and Jane and Spot and Puff couldn't hold a candle to Jack and the Beanstalk and Red Riding Hood and Pooh and Peter Rabbit, then many, many children *must* feel very much the same way, even though Dick and Jane have given way to Meg and Billy or any other string of "current" names. There is no substitute for *real* books. They are rarely boring or sanitized or squeezed into a "reading system" that children can smell a mile off. So logic says if we want *real* readers we must give them *real* books; give our young people good literature, good art, and, surprisingly, these young people may do the rest.

Tomie dePaola

Preface

Some books published by the International Reading Association are the result of a committee's work over a number of years; some represent the efforts of dedicated members who see gaps in the offerings and propose to fill them; some are responses to requests from the Publications Committee charged with overseeing the comprehensiveness of the publications program. This book, however, is the result of a request from Ronald Mitchell, Executive Director of the International Reading Association.

Dr. Mitchell, an astute observer of IRA members' needs, asked me, "Don't you think it's time IRA did something about children's literature and reading programs?" My natural response was, "Yes, of course it is." His next question was, "Will you help?" I delayed a response until I could check with the outstanding leaders in children's literature and reading. I found authors who were willing to contribute to such a project, and together we developed a plan and submitted a proposal to the Director of Publications and the Publications Committee.

This book, then, is dedicated to Ronald Mitchell, who requested it, and to all the teachers who want to use children's literature in their reading programs. This book is intended to help them decide which books to start with and how to use them with readers.

The first section is devoted to *why*: Why do we need children's literature in the reading program? Chapters by Bernice Cullinan and Bill Martin attempt to answer that question and to provide a rationale for using children's literature. A chapter by Nancy Larrick offers poetry as an invitation to reading at all levels.

The second section describes reading programs that use literature in the primary grades (K-3). Charlotte Huck and Kristen Kerstetter show how one school uses literature in kindergarten with developing readers. Linda Lamme describes an approach to teaching reading using whole language routines, including reading aloud, chanting from charts, book discussions, and writing.

Children's literature in the intermediate grades (4 to 6) is discussed in the third section, in three chapters devoted to various ways children can expand their reading skills. Rudine Sims Bishop describes specific books that can be used to develop multicultural understanding. Dorothy Strickland explains two major strategies that can be generalized across many books. Sam Sebesta vividly portrays using children's books to introduce children to the humanities, including drama, visual arts, movement, and writing.

The fourth section deals with children's literature in the upper grades (6 to 8). Dianne Monson provides ideas for engaging readers with realistic and historical fiction. Jean Greenlaw and Margaret McIntosh describe science fiction and fantasy that lead readers to develop their creative thinking. Both chapters are filled with practical ideas for teaching.

The final section encompasses the broader contexts in which literature is used to teach reading. Ira Aaron suggests how specific children's books can be integrated into a basic reading program. Lee Indrisano and Jean Paratore discuss using children's literature with disabled readers. Francie Alexander describes a statewide program of reading improvement being used in California. Arlene Pillar describes the many resources for locating children's literature of high quality.

Ideas developed by Lee Galda for teaching higher order reading skills are interspersed throughout the book.

This book may differ in tone from other books on reading instruction you have read. Our goal was to make our subject approachable through an informal writing style that sounds as if we were talking to you. The writing style, therefore, is casual and conversational, more often anecdotal than solemn.

We have heard many teachers say they would use literature in the reading program if they knew which books to use and what to do with them. These are the teachers to whom this book is addressed.

This book does not attempt to provide a comprehensive reading program; that would take far more coordination and planning than is possible for professionals working independently. It is, however, intended to be a beginning–a jumping off place–for teachers who know that the magic of a good story can engage readers, keep them reading, and help them discover the joy we experience from reading ourselves.

Bernice E. Cullinan
New York, 1987

Contributors

Ira E. Aaron
University of Georgia (Emeritus)
Athens, Georgia

Francie Alexander
California State Department of Education
Sacramento, California

Rudine Sims Bishop
The Ohio State University
Columbus, Ohio

Bernice E. Cullinan
New York University
New York, New York

Lee Galda
University of Georgia
Athens, Georgia

M. Jean Greenlaw
North Texas State University
Denton, Texas

Charlotte S. Huck
The Ohio State University
Columbus, Ohio

Roselmina Indrisano
Boston University
Boston, Massachusetts

Kristen Jeffers Kerstetter
Highland Park School
Grove City, Ohio

Linda Leonard Lamme
University of Florida
Gainesville, Florida

Nancy Larrick
Winchester, Virginia

Bill Martin Jr
New York, New York

Margaret E. McIntosh
North Texas State University
Denton, Texas

Dianne L. Monson
University of Minnesota
Minneapolis, Minnesota

Jeanne R. Paratore
Boston University
Boston, Massachusetts

Arlene M. Pillar
Long Beach, New York

Sam Leaton Sebesta
University of Washington
Seattle, Washington

Dorothy S. Strickland
Teachers College
Columbia University
New York, New York

IRA DIRECTOR OF PUBLICATIONS   Jennifer A. Stevenson

IRA PUBLICATIONS COMMITTEE 1986-1987   James E. Flood, San Diego State University, *Chair* • James F. Baumann, Purdue University • Janet R. Binkley, IRA • Rudine Sims Bishop, The Ohio State University • Carl Braun, University of Calgary • Susan W. Brennan, IRA • Richard L. Carner, University of Miami • Richard C. Culyer III, Coker College • Dolores Durkin, University of Illinois • Philip Gough, University of Texas at Austin • John Micklos, IRA • Ronald W. Mitchell, IRA • Joy N. Monahan, Orange County Public Schools, Orlando, Florida • Allan R. Neilsen, Mount St. Vincent University • John J. Pikulski, University of Delaware • María Elena Rodríguez, IRA, Buenos Aires • Robert Schreiner, University of Minnesota • Jennifer A. Stevenson, IRA

The International Reading Association attempts, through its publications, to provide a forum for a wide spectrum of opinions on reading. This policy permits divergent viewpoints without assuming the endorsement of the Association.

Section 1

Children's Literature: Invitation to Reading

Why do we need children's literature in the reading program? The first two chapters in this section attempt to answer that question by providing a rationale and showing some of the benefits of using literature. Bernice Cullinan claims that it takes a good story to hold readers' interest and to teach reading comprehension. She also shows how reading good literature affects children's use of language in speaking and writing. Bill Martin describes the lasting effects of a teacher's influence and the role that literature played in shaping his life's work. He reveals some of the features of language he considers important as he writes books for children or selects ones to use with them. To conclude the section, Nancy Larrick's chapter on poetry in the reading program appears as an invitation to reading to show that poetry permeates good practice at all levels.

Chapter 1

Inviting Readers to Literature

Bernice E. Cullinan

Ellie Kazin's third grade students are known all over town. School and public librarians know them because they bombard the libraries asking for books. The grocer knows them because they come into the store asking for empty cartons to make into puppet theaters. The principal knows them because they're found reading in hallways, alcoves, and classrooms. One student has read all of Charlotte Zolotow's books and is a Zolotow expert; another is a specialist in Ezra Jack Keats; another specializes in Maurice Sendak. Why is this so? Because their teacher has set fire to their enthusiasm for reading. She has not only taught them how to read; she has made them want to read.

There are at least two goals for every school reading program: (1) to teach students how to read and (2) to make them want to read. We have been reasonably successful with the first goal, less so with the second. Good literature in the reading program can help us make students want to read.

Why Do We Need Good Literature in the Reading Program?

To document the need for literature in the reading program, I went to the experts, and here is what I heard them say.

It Takes a Good Story

I asked Dorsey Hammond, teacher educator from Oakland University, why he thought it was important to have good literature in the reading program. He replied, "Well, you can't teach reading comprehension if you don't have a good story to work with." He went on to say that by the time they're five or six, most children have a well developed sense of story; they have expectations of what a story should be—we call it their story schema (Anderson & Pearson, 1984). Since comprehension is shaped by the reader's schema—the knowledge already stored in memory about what *should* be—it stands to reason that when new material conforms to expectations, it is easier to understand. When the new information is combined with prior knowledge, we call it comprehension. Comprehending a story is like completing a puzzle–all of the information is used; it fits together without forcing. Good literature contains well crafted elements which create a coherent picture and which support logical inferences. Good stories provide reading teachers with the right materials to teach reading comprehension. Students remember and are quick to recall good literature; they store it in their memories and draw upon it to comprehend new information.

Nancy Curtin, the children's librarian in my local library, faced the last story hour before the Christmas break. She scanned the shelves for a good Christmas story, but found to her dismay that all the seasonal stories had been checked out. She did find a copy of a supermarket book about Santa Claus left in the lost and found bin. "Surely," she thought, "they'll like a Santa Claus story even if it may not be a very strong one."

Nancy began the story hour with some favorite songs, finger plays, and rhymes to bring the eager children to rapt attention. Then she read aloud the Santa Claus book, expecting their attention to continue. She was surprised when an obvious change of mood occurred; the children became restless and

*Illustration from **The Polar Express** by Chris Van Allsburg. Copyright © 1985 by Chris Van Allsburg. Reprinted by permission of Houghton Mifflin Company.*

started talking to one another instead of listening to the book. They looked bewildered, as if to say, "Why are you reading this?" Nancy said, "There was absolutely no 'story' in the book; it was a series of incidents involving the man in the red suit." When she finished, she quickly grabbed an old favorite, *Sylvester and the Magic Pebble* by William Steig, and the children immediately became attentive again. Nancy said, "Children know the difference; they won't sit still for a pointless, namby-pamby story." Now she tucks away a copy of *The Elves and the Shoemaker* (Littledale), *The Polar Express* (Van Allsburg), *On Christmas Eve* (Brown), *The Night Before Christmas* (Moore), or *Morris' Disappearing Bag* (Wells) so that she will not be caught short again.

Suzanne, an eighth grade student in a New York City school, said, "The first thing I expect when I read is that I expect to be drawn into the story and not know where I am. If I'm sitting here and I know that I'm sitting here looking at words on a page, then I'll just put the book down and not read it at all. I despise pushing myself at a book. If someone says, 'Read this,' and it's really awful, I'd just rather put it down. I really hate pushing myself through a book, being made to read a book I don't like. I fall into books the way some people fall into television."

Suzanne expresses her need for a story that captures her attention, one that transports her into the world of the story so she believes she is living in that world. A boy in Georgia expressed the same need by saying, "I want a story that inhales me."

I wonder if these are some of the reasons I could not get my hands on Judy Blume's book *Blubber*. The year it was published, I was a Regional Team Leader for the International Reading Association/Children's Book Council Children's Choices Project, and I circulated the books in city and suburban schools. Every time I visited a classroom, I heard the students talking about *Blubber*, and I was dying to read it myself. I asked one of the students for the book. She said, "Well, Nancy has it now but she promised to give it to Beth when she's done, then after that Zoe gets it, then Lisa, and then Nicole, and then ME! Maybe next time you come you can have it." But the story was the same on my next visit; only the list of readers changed. I never got my hands on the book until the project was over and I bought a copy at my local bookstore. The fourth grade students whispered, "We really do act like the people in *Blubber*, but we know we shouldn't. Could Judy Blume eavesdrop and hear us talking? How could she know?" Seeing such a true picture of themselves captured their interest and kept them spellbound.

Students Absorb the Language of Literature

Language is one of the primary instruments we use to interpret and organize our experience; it helps us understand our world and our place in it. Halliday (1982) says that we use language to build a picture of the world–not only the world in which we live but, also, the world of our consciousness and imagination.

Young children use language to make sense of their world; they often express their perceptions in vivid images to explain how things seem to them. After collecting hundreds of examples of things children said, Chukovsky (1971) concluded that children are linguistic geniuses; for example, "I'm barefoot all over." "Don't put out the light, I can't see how to sleep." "Granny, you are my best-be-loved." Children learn from the language they hear; it makes sense that the richer the language environment, the richer the language learning. Since the process of language learning continues throughout the school years, those years need to be filled with the storehouse of exciting words found in good literature.

Researchers show that children take over the language they hear and read and use it as part of their own (Cazden, 1972; Chomsky, 1972; White, 1954, 1984). For example, White's *Books before Five* is a journal of her daughter Carol's responses to books. Carol, intrigued with Potter's *The Tale of Peter Rabbit*, adopted some of the phrases from the book into her speech and conversation. On one occasion Carol began using admonishments that she would not have heard in her family. Her mother writes:

> I've just realized that into my normal cautions she has blended Mrs. Rabbit's "You may go into the fields and down the lane but don't go into Mr. McGregor's garden." Yesterday when I left her next door while I went to town she called back after me, "Mummy." Then, holding her head on one side and putting on the half-smiling, half-stern face which signals that she is acting, she said, "Don't go on the street cars, run over and get some buns, and don't go in Mr. McGregor's garden" (p. 45).

On another occasion Carol showed the same affinity for the language of Potter's story *The Tale of Mrs. Tiggy-Winkle*. Mrs. Tiggy-Winkle,

*Illustration from **The Tale of Peter Rabbit** by Beatrix Potter (Frederick Warne, 1902), copyright © 1902 by Frederick Warne & Co. Reprinted by permission.*

a hedgehog, is a meticulous washerwoman; she is terribly particular about her ironing. White says:

> After the reading was over I fed the baby while Carol spent the time (pretend) "ironing," a perfect Mrs. Tiggy-Winkle. She turned the word Tiggy-Winkle over on her tongue, with the usual pleasure she gets from polysyllables, (such as) "animals," "hospital," or "exciting." And as she ironed she repeated quietly, "Sometimes a hedgehog came by and sometimes a mouse" (p. 68).

Sometimes single words appear in children's conversations as they try out new ways of making meaning. Hallie was just three when she announced one morning that her breakfast bacon "crunched just like the sound Peter made in the snow in *The Snowy Day*" (Keats).

Young children like to play with the sounds of language. The lilting language of literature that falls softly on the ear lingers in the mind; it appears in our speech and writing. Children make literary language part of their own language because it is memorable.

A literature program provides strong language models. Hearing and reading good stories helps to develop vocabularies, sharpens a sensitivity to language, and fine tunes a sense of writing styles. Moffett (1968) says that what we draw upon in our own writing is determined by our prior verbal experience; our reading is a potent source of content and form for our writing. Smith (1982) goes further, saying the only source of knowledge sufficiently rich and reliable for learning about written language is the writing already done by others. He states that we learn to write by reading what others have written; we enrich our repertoire of ways to say things by reading what others have said. Nick Aversa, an English teacher in Great Neck South Middle School, said, "We read *My Life and Hard Times* by James Thurber, and then I saw aspects of Thurber's style cropping up in students' writing the rest of the year. The literature we read is actually a demonstration of good writing; students try on other writers' styles in the process of creating their own."

Literature Feeds the Fancy

Literature informs the imagination and feeds the desire to read. When students are surrounded with rich examples of the language of literature they develop a storehouse of images and story patterns to draw upon for their own expression. White (1954, 1984) describes how pretending was a natural part of Carol's life and how it is related to literature. Carol was read to on a regular basis and drew from her stories as well as from real life to create her games, as when she said, "You be the hunter and I'll be the wolf." Without hesitation, Carol and her friends assigned and played the parts of Goldilocks, Simple Simon, and Engineer Small. White says, "All the Mother Goose characters are more than jingles to her; they represent a world which overflows into her own...just as Dickens characters do with a Boz enthusiast" (p. 37). Characters from Carol's books popped in and out of her life at her whim.

How Can We Make Students Willing Readers?

Literature in a reading program does more than merely attract willing readers. Literature educates the imagination, provides language models, and molds the intellect. The heritage of humankind lies in books; we endow students with the key to their legacy when we teach them to read.

One classroom teacher said to me, "I

have no trouble using literature for storytime; I do that, but I have to teach the basic reading skills. My students are tested on standardized tests and I want them to pass them. I would use literature in the reading program if you could show me how to teach reading skills with it." Another who values literature for itself said, "I don't like to destroy the beauty of literature by using it to teach word attack skills, vocabulary development, and reading comprehension. How can I teach skills without ruining the literature?" These are the teachers we address in this book.

There is a fine line between using children's literature to teach reading skills and destroying the literature we use. For example, I

*Illustration from **Dear Mr. Henshaw** by Beverly Cleary, illustrated by Paul O. Zelinsky. Copyright © 1983 by Beverly Cleary. William Morrow and Company, Inc. Reprinted by permission.*

was not happy the day I saw children assigned to search a page of a favorite story for all the words that began with the letter *p*. I have no quarrel, however, with teachers of beginning reading who call attention to the structural elements of words or of a story once their students have enjoyed reading the story for its content. I was delighted to see a teacher using *Dear Mr. Henshaw* (Cleary) to teach students to make inferences. They discussed what Mr. Henshaw must have said in his replies to Leigh Botts; the students' responses were quite logical even though what Mr. Henshaw said is never stated in the text.

You don't need to ruin literature, such as teaching grammar through poetry, but you can base your teaching of higher level reading skills on children's literature. See the Teaching Ideas by Galda and other authors in this text for specific suggestions.

What Strategies Can I Use?

Shared reading. Shared reading is an approach for beginning reading that builds on the model of the bedtime story, in which an adult shares a book with a child (or a group of children) by reading it aloud and pointing to the words (Doake, 1985; Holdaway, 1979). Stories with predictable, rhythmic language work best; for example, *Mrs. Wishy-Washy* (Wright Story Box Program), *Noisy Nora* (Wells), and *Brown Bear, Brown Bear* (Martin).

When the bedtime story situation is transferred to the classroom, an adjustment must be made in the size of the book and print. A book that can be seen at close range by two or three children must be enlarged into an oversized book so an entire class group can see the pictures and the print. In the shared reading experience, children cluster around the big book. The teacher leads them through

When stories are shared through reading big books, many children can see the pictures at the same time.

the book, encouraging them to make predictions about the story based on what they see in the illustrations and asking lots of questions, such as "What do you think is happening? What might happen next?" Then the teacher reads the story aloud and points to the words. Next, the group reads the story through several times in unison, although some students may join in only on repetitive refrains. When students read aloud as a group, success is guaranteed for everyone, with no child humiliated by lack of ability. As children repeatedly hear the words and see the print, they make associations between letters and sounds; many children figure out the code by themselves. Teachers ask students to point to words that begin alike or ones that have similar parts; phonics is taught in context, not in isolation.

Several regular sized copies of the same book should be available so children can re-read them on their own during free time or planned individualized reading time. Teachers could also tape record the book and have the cassette available for use at listening stations.

Shared reading also works well beyond the primary grades when teachers invite students to talk about books they read. Janice Henderson, one of the teachers reading specialist Hilda Lauber took me to visit in Baytown, Texas, had the students present "Book Sales," commercials in which students tried to sell the books they had read to others in the class. Some of the booksellers dressed up as the main characters in their books, and some prepared posters or other props. They were careful as they talked about books so they would not give away the ending. Some students sat on the edges of their chairs ready to grab a book so they could read it next.

Another teacher used a file box for student reactions to books they read.

Reading aloud. Enthusiasm for reading spreads like wildfire when teachers are excited about it. Teachers have a potentially tremendous effect; they are the models. The teacher who reads aloud is doing what Jim Trelease, author of *The Read-Aloud Handbook,* calls advertising. The oral reader is saying, "Listen to this! There's great stuff in these books, and you can have it just by reading!" Reading aloud should not stop when students learn to read on their own. They need to see rewards for applying some of the skills they have learned.

Some of my most pleasant memories of school surround my seventh grade English teacher who read aloud to us every day. I can still almost hear the book crackle as she opened it and smoothed its pages, heightening the anticipation as we settled in for the next chapter. She always made the story sound so good I couldn't wait to read it on my

File Box of Books Children Have Read

- Use a 3 x 5 inch (or larger) file box to create a file of books.
- When students finish reading a book, they should make a file card for the book, including the following information:
  - Author and title.
  - Where the book can be found.
  - Two or three sentences about the book. (Don't give away the plot.)
  - Evaluation: I liked/did not like it. I would/would not recommend it to others.
- Students should consult the file when they are looking for a book to read.

Adapted from an idea by Sandra Maccarone, Orlando, Florida

Teaching Idea

Biography Project

- Have students select a biography to read, but keep the name of the subject a secret. While they are reading, they should cover the book with brown paper so others will not see the subject's name.
- After they finish reading, students will need to select clues about subjects' identities. Model the process for them by reading a biography aloud and then choosing clues as a group.
- Have students prepare a list of ten clues about the identity of each subject.
- Using the clues the class prepared for the biography read aloud, demonstrate how to arrange the clues from the most difficult to those that nearly give away the subject's identity.
- Have students arrange the clues from the most difficult to the easiest for their subjects.
- On an appointed day, ask students to come prepared to present their clues to the rest of the class. They may wear or carry something characteristic of their subjects.
- One at a time, have students read clues to the class, starting with the most difficult, until their classmates guess the person.
- At the end of the project, each student should write a biography of a classmate, choosing subjects in consultation with the teacher.
- Student biographies may be published in the school newspaper.

Adapted from an idea by Zora Brown, Little Red Schoolhouse, New York

own. I realize now that she was modeling–modeling good oral reading and showing us what wonderful stories lay in books. Her enthusiasm was contagious.

Reading groups. Teachers who use literature with ability level reading groups sometimes find that multiple copies of stories are not available. More teachers would use literature if they could stop by the school library or office and say, "I am starting a unit on courage. Could I have ten copies of three different books on that theme at my students' reading level?" In some cases, the solution to this may be as simple as selecting books available in less expensive paperback editions.

At the same time, teachers often say they cannot find time for Sustained Silent Reading. They have solved the problem in a variety of ways. For example, when the teacher is working with one group, members of the other groups can be reading on their own. A teacher in New Jersey cut five minutes a day from each reading group to get fifteen additional minutes, then added fifteen minutes more from other activities to give the students thirty minutes of silent reading a day. She even found time in that thirty minute period to confer quietly with each student at least once a week.

When students are taught reading in basic reading programs, they need to learn that

Compare Different Versions of the Same Story

- Books: *Beauty* by Robin McKinley and any version of *Beauty and the Beast.*
  McKinley expanded the folktale into a full length novel. Her version is gripping, even though you know how the story comes out.
- Read aloud *Beauty.*
- Ask students to read the folktale version of *Beauty and the Beast* (de Beaumont).
- Compare the two versions.
  - Who are the main characters?
  - What do you know about them?
  - How does the language of the two versions differ?
  - What do you know about the settings?
  - Do the versions differ in how much is shown and how much is told about what is happening?
  - How does McKinley expand an event in the story? Give an example.
  - Compare the amount of writing it takes to tell an episode in the folktale version with McKinley's retelling. In this case, is shorter necessarily better?

reading has an application beyond the book they are using. One application is pleasure reading (discussed earlier) but there are other applications as well. Students might practice their skills in research projects in which they track down what a number of different writers have to say about an issue.

Building a Literate Nation

Although the United States is becoming a nation of readers, this is true for only part of the population. A Book Industry Study Group survey shows that 80 percent of all books read are read by only 10 percent of the people. The survey also shows a decline in book readers in the age group under 21, from 75 percent in 1978 to 63 percent in 1983. We can turn those figures around. When students are invited to read good children's literature, they partake eagerly of the feast.

A new term has been generated to describe a condition prevalent in our society today. That term is aliteracy; an aliterate is a person who knows how to read but who doesn't choose to read. These are people who glance at the headlines of a newspaper and grab the TV schedule. They do not read books for pleasure, nor do they read extensively for information. An aliterate is not much better off than an illiterate, a person who cannot read at all. Aliterates miss the great novels of the past and present. They also miss probing analyses written about political issues. Most aliterates watch television for their news, but the entire transcript of a television newscast fills only two columns of a newspaper such as *The New York Times* or *The Washington Post*. Aliterates get only the surface level of the news.

Providing Time to Read

Students need a lot of practice to become skilled readers. The old saying "Practice makes perfect" applies to reading as much as it does to anything else. Learning to read is like learning to play the piano: The more we practice, the better we become. *Becoming a Nation of Readers* (Anderson et al., 1985) shows that students who read most read best. The National Assessment of Educational Progress shows that the amount of reading done out of school is consistently related to gains in reading achievement as measured by standardized tests.

One group of researchers had fifth grade students keep a daily log of after school activities for several months (Anderson et al., 1985). Fifty percent of the fifth graders read books an average of 4 minutes per day or less, 30 percent read 2 minutes per day or less, and 10 percent never reported reading any book on any day. For the majority of children, reading from books occupied 1 percent or less of their free time. In contrast, they averaged 130 minutes per day watching TV. Among all the ways students reported spending their leisure time, average minutes per day reading books was the best predictor of reading comprehension, vocabulary size, and gains in reading achievement between second and fifth grades. The overall results showed, however, that students didn't read very much during their free time. What does this mean for teachers? I think it means we must give them time to read in school.

Learning about Literature Ourselves

Ellie Kazin says she signed up at Adelphi University for the course in children's literature thinking that it would be interesting, but never realizing how expansive the possibilities were to do things with literature in her own classroom. Something magical happened in Barbara Goldman's course: The teachers who were her students developed a passion for books. Instead of sneaking out early to drive the thirty miles to her home as she had planned, Ellie stayed beyond the two hour session to discuss further ideas with her classmates. She carried her enthusiasm back to her classroom. When Barbara Goldman asked for annotations of thirty easy picture books, analyses of text and illustrations, memorable vocabulary, and connecting themes to other books, Ellie took the assignment to her third graders and said, "I'm learning about books and this is what I'll be doing. Come learn with me. We'll take this course together." Students wrote annotations.

Barbara Goldman applauded the close connection between university work and classroom activity; she periodically visited the classroom. The students also corresponded with her, happy to be doing "college" work. When she assigned comparisons of variants of folktales, Ellie again turned the assignment over to her students. They searched for variants and wrote their own versions of folktales. For the informational books assignment, they cleared the library shelves of math books and created board games to illustrate their reading. The school librarian was impressed with their broad reading and told them so. Ellie Kazin's students will never forget the pleasure they generated for themselves by this shared experience.

Goldman believes that this kind of simultaneous learning ought to be a regular part of staff development because it achieves six laudable goals:

1. The children see their teacher as an active participant in the year long activity of reading many books from the library.

2. The books themselves appear "ageless." For example, the artistry of Maurice Sendak or William Steig is as suitable for the aesthetic senses of an adult as for a child.

3. A great deal of sharing takes place among students as they write annotations and perceive themselves to be experts on authors, themes, types of poetry, and variants of folktales.

4. The entire library becomes a potential reading source; children select material according to their own interests and at their own reading levels.

5. Students and teachers develop a respect for the body of work of a writer or illustrator. For example, the connections among the many works of Leo Lionni become apparent if they are read extensively.

6. Teachers and students begin to see connections among different writers and recognize the universality of their themes. For example, courage, friendship, loss, and triumph over adversity can be found in many books. When reading one book and seeing connections to another book, the mind of a child or an adult has been challenged to "think a new thought."

The more teachers know about literature, the more they will find ways to incorporate the books they cherish into an already crowded schedule. Wise teachers know that literature enriches a curriculum when it is integrated into every area. Goldman paraphrases Robert Frost: "One could do worse than be a reader of children's books."

As you teach children to read, share with them in many ways the magic contained in children's literature. They will then want to read and you will have succeeded twice.

In Summary

It takes a good story to teach reading comprehension and to hold a reader's interest.

Students learn the language of literature by reading and hearing literature read aloud.

Students draw upon what they read as a source of knowledge when they write.

Teachers can demonstrate their enthusiasm for reading through shared reading, reading aloud, and reading in groups.

Students who read a lot become fluent readers.

Enthusiasm for reading is contagious.

References

Anderson, Richard C., Hiebert, Elfrieda H., Scott, Judith A., and Wilkinson, Ian A.G. *Becoming a nation of readers: The report of the commission on reading.* Washington, D.C.: National Institute of Education, 1985.

Anderson, Richard C., and Pearson, P. David. A schema-theoretic view of basic processes in reading comprehension. In P. David Pearson (Ed.), *Handbook of reading research.* New York: Longman, 1984.

Book Industry Study Group. *The 1983 consumer research study on reading and book purchasing.* New York: Book Industry Study Group, 1984.

Cazden, Courtney. *Child language and education.* New York: Holt, 1972.

Chomsky, Carol. Stages in language development and reading exposure. *Harvard Educational Review,* 1972, 1-33.

Chukovsky, Kornei. *From two to five.* Translated by M. Norton. Berkeley: University of California Press, 1971.

Doake, David. Reading-like behavior: Its role in learning to read. In A. Jaggar and M.T. Smith-Burke (Eds.), *Observing the language learner.* Newark, DE: International Reading Association, 1985, 82-98.

Halliday, M.A.K. Three aspects of children's language development: Learning language, learning through language, learning about language. In Y. Goodman, M. Haussler, and D. Strickland (Eds.), *Oral and written language development research: Impact on the schools.* Urbana, IL: National Council of Teachers of English, 1982.

Holdaway, Don. *The foundations of literacy.* Portsmouth, NH: Heinemann, 1979.

Moffett, James. *Teaching the universe of discourse.* Boston: Houghton Mifflin, 1968.

Smith, Frank. *Writing and the writer.* New York: Holt, 1982.

Trelease, Jim. *The read-aloud handbook,* revised edition. New York: Viking Penguin, 1985.

White, Dorothy. *Books before five.* Portsmouth, NH: Heinemann, 1954, 1984.

Children's Books

Blume, Judy. *Blubber.* Bradbury, 1974.

Brown, Margaret Wise. *On Christmas Eve.* Childrens, 1961.

Cleary, Beverly. *Dear Mr. Henshaw.* Morrow, 1983.

de Beaumont, Madame. *Beauty and the Beast.* Bradbury, 1978 (1740).

Keats, Ezra Jack. *The Snowy Day.* Viking, 1962.

Littledale, Freya. *The Elves and the Shoemaker.* Illustrated by Brinton Turkle, Scholastic, 1975.

Martin Bill Jr. *Brown Bear, Brown Bear.* Illustrated by Eric Carle. Holt, 1983.

McKinley, Robin. *Beauty: A Retelling of the Story of Beauty and the Beast.* Harper, 1978.

Moore, Clement C. *The Night Before Christmas.* Illustrated by Tomie dePaola. Holiday House, 1980.

Potter, Beatrix. *The Tale of Peter Rabbit.* Warne, 1902.

Potter, Beatrix. *The Tale of Mrs. Tiggy-Winkle.* Warne, 1905.

Steig, William. *Sylvester and the Magic Pebble.* Simon and Schuster, 1969.

Thurber, James. *My Life and Hard Times.* Harper and Row, 1973.

Van Allsburg, Chris. *The Polar Express.* Houghton Mifflin, 1985.

Wells, Rosemary. *Morris' Disappearing Bag.* Dial, 1975.

Wells, Rosemary. *Noisy Nora* (Big Book). Scholastic, 1976.

Wright Story Box Program. *Mrs. Wishy-Washy.* Wright Group Publishing, 1984.

Chapter 2
The Making of a Reader: A Personal Narrative

Bill Martin Jr

A blessed thing happened to me as a child. I had a teacher who read to me. Of course she was reading to all other children in the classroom, but I believed she was reading *just to me* because I was a nonreader.

Miss Davis read aloud several times a day that fifth grade year. Always a chapter or two from the ongoing book chosen for its relevancy. Always a poem or two which she had catalogued in memory or in a book for instant retrieval. Sometimes a short story or two in lieu of the chapter from the ongoing book.

She read to us three times a day unless we were cantankerous, for which one of the reading times was eliminated. Missing a read-aloud was too great a price to pay for "busting out" at the mental seams, so we were what was called a "good" class. We geared to the continuing pulse of literary adventure.

The first read-aloud occurred at the opening of each day, just after the singing of "America" and giving the flag salute. Without comment Miss Davis picked up the book, turned to the appropriate page, and moist-

ened her lips as if fueling up for a long trip. We kids soon came to attention, awaiting "take-off." When Miss Davis started reading, our meager hold on the day became solvent, and we adventured victoriously through the webbings of language, catching glimpses of ourselves within the story. At the same time we were neutralized of any excesses and anxieties we had brought into the classroom. It was a good start for the school day.

The second read-aloud came just after noontime (called "dinnertime" in those days) which always terminated in a swirl of noisy, sweaty, rambunctious behavior that had to be dealt with prior to afternoon lessons. As in the morning, literature was the Pied Piper as well as the exorcist.

Just before afternoon dismissal, Miss Davis read again to dispel, I'm sure, the stress inculcated by school routine. It was as if she wanted us to go home free of education's threatened damnations and open to family pleasures and responsibilities.

Those three daily read-alouds proved to be my "basic" education. They kept me in sync with my dreams of "amounting to something" when I "grew up." They provided the literary touchstone that has sustained all of my life.

If Miss Davis knew that I was not a reader, she never mentioned it. I was wholesomely at home in the classroom. Learning wasn't as specialized then as it is now. There were no classes for the less able kids. Neither were there classes for the gifted. We were all of a group, a pack, sharing individual triumphs and misfortunes in common cause.

I had been well schooled to survive as a nonreader. All through the grades teachers complimented my ability to draw, to ride the crest of the day. They appreciated my willingness, my cheerfulness, my rosy cheeks. There were no reading tests beyond the teacher's interrogations, and I was skillful at catching the drift of the conversation and classroom comments which could be woven into a reasonable answer to a question. Had I been born thirty years later, the school, with its fetish for reading skills, probably would have divorced me from eventually coming to print. Fortunately, like Leo (*Leo the Late Bloomer*, Kraus), I was nurtured for late blooming.

My first book reading came when I was twenty. In college. Yes, then even nonreaders were admitted to college or university if they could muster tuition fees. By this time in my life I was so skilled in masking my print blindness that most teachers thought I was lazy, unprepared, never suspecting that it was my ears, not my eyes, that opened Sesame. I have Miss Davis to thank. She tuned my ears to literate language, to the voice of the text. Not to the voice of Jack London, but to the voice of his story, "To Build a Fire." Not to the voice of Robert Louis Stevenson, but to the voice of *Treasure Island.* Not to the voice of James

Whitcomb Riley, but to the voice of "Little Orphant Annie." Not to the voice of Daniel DeFoe, but to the voice of *Robinson Crusoe.* Now, years later, I have learned to search the page for the voice of the text in determining whether to devote reading time to an unfamiliar book. In this context, *voice* and *comprehension* are synonymous.

The miracle of Miss Davis was that she knew the difference between teaching and infusion. Between skillbuilding and learning. Between test scores and life. She, to my knowledge, never verbalized these differences. She lived them. As Henry Miller said of one of his early teachers, it was not her view of reading but her view of life that made books so important.

I remember, for instance, that in the midst of reading Emerson Hough's long forgotten book, *North of Thirty-Six,* Miss Davis commented without elaboration that the hero of the story was not the cowboy but the herd of cattle. That I still remember it is tribute to insightfulness of a book-oriented, language-loving teacher.

Before she started reading Palmer Cox's *The Brownies,* she placed the book on the library shelf for several days, giving us each a chance to explore its pictorial maze and amazements. "The pictures are better than the book," she observed. "The pictures flow, the story rhymes are stilted." *The Brownies* is the first book I ever read, albeit with pictures. It still is on my list of favorites.

When, in Stevenson's *Treasure Island,* Jim Hawkins and his mother went back into the fearsome darkness of the Admiral Benbow Inn to take due payment from the purse of lifeless Old Sea Dog, a peg-legged pirate, she said, "This was an act demanding courage that few have but all hope to have." She was always interspersing comments and questions that helped us distance ourselves from the text, but at the same time lose ourselves in its relevancies.

Reading aloud was integral in her ambitions for us kids. Miss Davis never missed a day reading to us. When we begged her to continue a reading session, she often complied, knowing (as children do), that a good story refuses to be left alone. It keeps nagging one to continue. That kind of nagging is life's most pleasant reading instruction.

Paul Witty, my second mentor, since deceased but increasingly a better friend and stronger influence in my life, ignored the reading skills in favor of children's interests as the key to getting involved with books. Once the natural and pervasive concerns of a child are known, he said, a child can be wooed to print with books that feed the abiding appetites. Children, like adults, find a way to read anything and everything that dovetails with life's ongoingness.

Peggy Brogan was my third and foremost mentor. I encountered her when I first came to New York to edit reading materials for the classroom. Peggy's steadfast faith in children's ability to deal with encoding and decoding print was contagious. I caught it out of the atmosphere. And it became a reality. As a child once said after her breakthrough to reading, "I'm not stuck anymore!" So was I freed not only in creating books for children but also in my expectations of what children would do with those books. My metamorphosis was complete: The nonreader had become a reader, the reader had become a writer, the writer had become a teacher.

With similar insight and confidence Frank Smith (1973, 1978) counsels that *children learn to read by reading. Just reading. More. And more. And more.* The message is clear. Reading instruction has less to do with skills than with luring children to book experiences - touch-and-go books, try-this-one-for-size, here's-a-tale-just-for-you - necessary beachheads for both the able and the frail in their quest for books that tap their dreams.

A child interested in snakes, for example, soon outruns easy-to-read books on the subject and, out of self-established purpose, delves into more complicated writings. Even those books obviously tailored to the mature mind. What the child can't read is sometimes skipped but more often conjectured. Using a rangy set of clues. Manageable sentences. Triggering words. Illuminating phrases. Pictorials. Personal experiences. Stored knowledge. Remembered feelings. Determined effort. Cross referencing. Sudden recognitions. But mostly common sense. Consciously and intuitively the child is developing a solid base of functional reading skills.

And at some point in this roundelay of reader-writer-text conferencing and messaging, the continuing reader quietly takes over the responsibility of making sense out of text. This occurs without fanfare. Without pronouncement. The reader becomes the teacher. The questioner and the responder. Free to risk. To test. To hunch. And to conclude. In a way similar to the phenomenon of learning to talk, the emergent reader is supported by the collective memory and enthusiasms of others in home and classroom, by the constant modeling and subtle beckonings of child-respecting, book-loving, print-oriented adults.

Children naturally gravitate to those books on the reading table that they can sail through, having heard them read aloud and chorused so frequently that they are etched into long term memory. Books such as Leland Jacobs's classic *Goodnight Mr. Beetle,* Christina Rosetti's poem, *"What Is Pink?"*, presented as a picture book, and the ever-intriguing always-renewing *"The Old Woman and Her Pig"* (Galdone). Children's success as readers of "whole books" turns them first into their own press agents, "Hey, I can read this book all by myself!" and soon after into proud critics of their reading experiences, "This is the best book I ever read!"

Once they sense their emerging power over the printed page, children find new respect for the joys of reading and for the need to read. Concomitantly they are enlarging their dreams of adventuring through a challenging range of depth of books, with increased confidence that they can successfully grapple with the autonomous language of a book to find its personal relevancy. *When this awareness occurs, a lifetime of reading follows.*

Reading now is by osmosis. Without consciousness of how and why. Without identifying which skills are needed or which are being used. The reader is forever rummaging and scavenging through the pages for a glimpse of self. For a vote of validation. For the pleasure of finding a closer relationship of the outer world to the inner world and vice versa. For the intense satisfaction of finding a special book that speaks to both the heart and the mind.

The California Reading Initiative promises a rich resource of children's books in every classroom, a necessary requisite to a mass development of lifelong readers. Twelve percent of the state's educational budget has been hallmarked for book purchases other than textbooks, thereby freeing children to create their own reading themes as they individually pursue their abiding and emerging interests. The program invites teachers to spend time in reading aloud and summarizing old favorites as well as newly published books; it also makes it permissible for children to read silently and to one another for the pure joy and intrigue of reading, improving the quality of language and therefore *life* itself.

Imagine the radiant expectancy of children and teachers discovering the literary flow and impact of *Whose Mouse Are You?* by Robert Kraus. It's the perfect novel for four, five, and six year olds. A Dickensian novel, if you please, with an unforgettable hero who overcomes life's bleakest moments with courage, inventiveness, and steadfast love worthy of our emulation. It is told in the polished prose of poetry that indelibly impresses itself in long term memory for a lifetime of repetitions, transformations, and appreciations, and it is published in picture book form for instant replays now, tomorrow, or forty years hence. It is the ultimate at one's command.

Then contemplate the expanded joy when the same children and teachers discover that there is a second Little Mouse adventure, *Where Are You Going, Little Mouse?* They are caught up in anticipation of even greater well being. Of renewed friendship. Of sharing new time and space with thoughts, concepts, and language that truly make a difference in one's life! It has nothing to do with IQ. Nothing to do with yesterday's failures. Nothing to do with reading. Yet it has everything to do with lifelong reading. And with the joy of learning.

Miss Davis would have been the first to have loved *Little Mouse.*

References

Smith, Frank. *Psycholinguistics and reading.* New York: Holt, Rinehart, and Winston, 1973.

Smith, Frank. *Reading without nonsense.* New York: Teachers College Press, 1978.

Children's Books

Cox, Palmer. *The Brownies: Their Book.* Dover, 1887.

Defoe, Daniel. *Robinson Crusoe.* Illustrated by Lynd Ward. Grosset & Dunlap, 1952-1963 (1719).

Galdone, Paul. *The Old Woman and Her Pig.* McGraw-Hill, 1961.

Hough, Emerson. *North of Thirty-Six.* Appleton, 1923.

Jacobs, Leland B. *Goodnight Mr. Beetle.* Illustrated by Gilbert Riswold. Holt, Rinehart and Winston, 1963.

Kraus, Robert. *Leo the Late Bloomer.* Illustrated by Jose Aruego. Windmill/Dutton, 1971.

Kraus, Robert. *Where Are You Going, Little Mouse?* Illustrated by Jose Aruego and Ariane Dewey. Greenwillow, 1986.

Kraus, Robert. *Whose Mouse Are You?* Illustrated by Jose Aruego. Macmillan, 1970.

London, Jack. "To Build a Fire." *The Youth's Companion,* 1902.

Riley, James Whitcomb. *Little Orphant Annie.* Putnam, 1983 (1908).

Rossetti, Christina. *What Is Pink?* Illustrated by Jose Aruego. Macmillan, 1971.

Stevenson, Robert Louis. *Treasure Island.* Illustrated by N.C. Wyeth. Scribner, 1981 (1883).

Chapter 3
Keep a Poem in Your Pocket

Nancy Larrick

I think the best suggestion for adults who meet regularly with children–at home or at school–is that of the poet Beatrice Schenk de Regniers: "Keep a poem in your pocket."

Have a poem ready for every mood, for every occasion. A poem to pull out on a rainy day when there can be no outdoor play. A poem to read when someone is feeling sad or discouraged. Or when a prevailing lethargy calls for a light touch or great guffaw. Often you will find a poem that adds richness to a prepared lesson: on the sun and the stars or on Indians of the Southwest or on Washington's Birthday.

Someone has likened the poem to the microchip: "A wealth of ideas in microspace." True, but the poem stirs human feelings and relationships as well.

Poems are different. Children are different. And situations vary from day to day. Introducing children and poetry means being flexible and ready to experiment. It means knowing the work of many poets and having those poems at your fingertips, if not in your memory bank. The introduction will be most effective if children have a part in selecting poems and devising ways by which they can hear the voice of the poet speaking to them personally.

I would hope that every child could meet some poetry every day–funny poems, touching poems, story poems, singing poems, bedtime poems–a wonderful assortment fitting into both planned and unplanned occasions.

Getting Children Involved

Like a song, a poem is meant to be heard. Children who have heard a poem many times, chiming in on repeated lines and perhaps adding sound effects and improvised musical accompaniment, are primed for reading the printed poem. Such children are eager and ready to read because they are familiar with the language, the melody, and the mood. Slow readers (even nonreaders) may be carried forward by the sounds of language that have become part of them.

For me, the most successful way to enlist children's enthusiasm for poetry is to get them involved in "doing a poem," as they put it. As an introduction, I often begin with folksongs and singing games that have lots of repetition. "London Bridge" is the perfect setup for a chorus and a small echo group to sing "falling down, falling down." The old spiritual "Kumba-ya" is another favorite for solo and chorus or solo and echo.

Once children are accustomed to group participation through song, they move happily to impromptu choral speaking of poetry. Only the leader needs words in print at this stage, for children are repeating and echoing what the leader reads. Nonreaders can participate easily and happily, thereby building their familiarity with the melody and vocabulary they will someday meet in print.

Many poems lend themselves easily to this kind of two or three part reading. For example, there are many question and answer poems such as "Who Made the Pie?" and "Did You Feed My Cow?" (from Wilner, *The Poetry Troupe*).

Poems with a chorus invite immediate participation, with a group of children chiming in after a solo reader. David McCord's "Riddle-Me Rhyme" (from McCord, *One at a Time*) gives double pleasure, with two choruses chanting one after the other throughout the tale of an owl beset by crows.

The poem with an echo, like the song with an echo, is always fun for group chanting. Eve Merriam's poem "Windshield Wiper" (from Merriam, *Out Loud*) gives almost identical lines of the two wipers echoing each other.

Sound effects and sound effect words frequently add to the dramatic appeal of a poem, and children like to chime in on these with their own voice effects or with created sound effects made with clicking pencils, tapping feet, or rhythm instruments.

Children delight in getting on their feet and moving as the poem directs. Patricia Hubbell provides for this beautifully in the poem "Bedtime" (from Hubbell, *8 A.M. Shadows*), which begins

Hop away
Skip away
Jump away
Leap!

"The Prayer of the Butterfly" by Carmen Bernos de Gasztold (from de Gasztold, *Prayers from the Ark*) gives very different directions. The words and the rhythm will set the children darting and whirling, tilting and flitting in butterfly fashion. When they hear "The Prayer of the Ox," children quickly change pace to the slow, heavy plodding of the ox. The rhythm guides them.

If you have moved to the rhythm of such poems as these, you soon realize that your whole body is helping you to feel the mood and the meaning of the poem.

Impromptu dramatization is still another kind of involvement children relish. Very young children learn to play the parts of Little Miss Muffet or Jack and Jill without rehearsal, costumes, or props.

Older children who revel in the humor of Shel Silverstein love to pantomime such poems as "Boa Constrictor" (from Silverstein, *Where the Sidewalk Ends*) or "Tryin' on Clothes" (from Silverstein, *A Light in the Attic*). As someone reads the lines, the mime takes over.

*Illustration from **A Light in the Attic,** poems and drawings by Shel Silverstein. Copyright © 1981 by Shel Silverstein. Harper and Row Publishers, Inc. Reprinted by permission.*

Ballads, old and new, suggest impromptu dramatization, often with sound effects: for example, "Get Up and Bar the Door," of ancient origin, and "The Old Wife and the Ghost" by James Reeves (both from Larrick, *Piping Down the Valleys Wild*).

As children become more involved physically–through impromptu choral reading, body movement, and dramatization–you will find them more at home with poetry and eager to read poetry in print. Gradually, they become emotionally as well as physically involved. As they make their voices harsh or tender, the language of the poem guides them from one mood to another.

I am convinced that children like an emotional tug. When they swirl and tilt with "The Prayer of the Butterfly," they, too, become joyous. And when they plod heavily with the ox, they feel the same weariness. They like to have their feelings stirred.

But What Does the Poem Mean?

So far I have spoken only of the joy of participating in a poem: the good feeling of snarling the "grinch grinch grunch"of the witch in "Listen" by Lilian Moore (from Cole, *A New Treasury of Children's Poetry*), of creating the musical sounds for "Tambourines" by Langston Hughes (from Larrick, *Tambourines! Tambourines to Glory!*), or the fun of imitating the crackles and growls of "Our Washing Machine" by Patricia Hubbell (from Hubbell, *The Apple Vendor's Fair*).

"But what does the poem mean?" is the follow up question many adults feel compelled to ask children. I have seen activity sheets asking children to write in the word or line from the poem that states the meaning or to make a choice in a multiple answer question about meaning, setting, people, or place.

Like scientists who resort to vivisection, we sometimes chop up a poem in order to pinpoint meaning. The end in both cases is a lifeless mess no one can enjoy.

Carl Sandburg (1930, p. 27) quotes an Irish philosopher as saying "What can be explained is not poetry." Sandburg continues, "There are people who want a book of verse to be like arithmetic–you turn to the back of the book and find the answers. Ken Nakazawa notes, 'The poems that are obvious are like the puzzles that are already solved. They deny us the joy of seeking and creating.'" Sandburg suggests that a poem leaves "something in the air for the reader of the poem to linger over."

At first glance, this may seem too general for children (and even for some adults) who want an exact answer–an answer that is not "up in the air." Acutally, we use poetic language every day and have done so for such a long time that we don't think of it as being poetry. It will help children if they become aware of these poetic words and phrases in everyday use. Consider the name of a flower such as *snapdragon* or *morning glory*. Each suggests and hints, but leaves us "the joy of seeking and creating."

To emphasize your point, bring to class a *tiger lily* or a spray of *bridle wreath* so children can see close up how appropriate these common names are–each suggesting a likeness in only one or two words.

Or consider the *weeping willow* tree and see how well this suggests the configuration of the tree. And when you are studying the stars and the planets, note the poetic term commonly used to describe the starry band that stretches across the heavens: *The Milky Way!* How much those words suggest about

an astronomical phenomenon! The meaning is clear even to the very young.

Children who have become aware of such picture making words in everyday use become sensitive to the understated language of the poet. They begin to look for hints suggesting more than is immediately apparent. They enjoy "seeking and creating."

Time for Poetry at Home

The Orlando, Florida, Public Library encourages parents to begin reading to their children at birth. Their slogan is "Catch 'em in the Cradle." They are convinced that parents should begin reading to their children in infancy. They want parents to know that children who are read to from birth grow to love reading more readily than those who are not read to.

Even infants respond to the sound of the human voice, and within a few months they begin to smile and wave their arms and legs to the rhythm of a song or poem. Then comes clapping to one of the old nursery songs such as "Tom, Tom, the Piper's Son." After hearing some of the old rhymes and songs again and again, a child will often chime in on a repeated word with the utmost delight.

Children who have had these experiences day after day come to kindergarten with a larger vocabulary than those who have not been read to and who have not been involved in poetry. Their facility with oral language, gained through listening to and then chanting poetry, becomes the foundation for reading at school.

This is only the start. Poetry at home can be an ongoing experience that fits into almost every facet of the child's life. For young children, there are countless poems about

Illustration from ***When the Dark Comes Dancing: A Bedtime Poetry Book*** compiled by Nancy Larrick, illustrated by John Wallner. Illustrations copyright © 1983 by John Wallner. Philomel Books, a division of The Putnam Publishing Group. Reprinted by permission.

playtime. "Sitting in the Sand" and "Hughbert and the Glue" by Karla Kuskin (from Kuskin, *Dogs & Dragons, Trees & Dreams*), "Skating Songs" and "The Box" by Myra Cohn Livingston (from Livingston, *A Song I Sang to You*), "Mine" and "Bike Ride" by Lilian Moore (from Moore, *Something New Begins*).

For all ages, there are spooky poems, such as "Skeleton Parade" by Jack Prelutsky and "The Goblin" by Rose Fyleman (both from Cole, *A New Treasury of Children's Poetry*). Collections of funny poems include *Where the Sidewalk Ends* and *A Light in the Attic* by Shel Silverstein, *My Tang's Tungled and Other*

Ridiculous Situations by Sara Brewton et al., and *They've Discovered a Head in the Box for the Bread and Other Laughable Limericks* compiled by John E. Brewton and Lorraine Blackburn.

There are poems to needle TV addicts; for hikers and surfers; for festive times and times to be alone and think things through. Poems about growing old and dying. Poems about family quarrels and disruption. Poems that look to the mountains or take you to the beach at sunrise.

Many parents will enjoy these poems as much as their children once they learn to become involved for sheer delight. But parents may need help from teachers and librarians in finding the poems and in using them with children.

Once they realize the pleasures of poetry day in and day out–what some call "Poetry Power"–they will be ready to share the poems children bring home and perhaps find others to add to the school collection.

Poetry at School

Poetry can fit into every part of the school day, adding the personal magnetism so often lacking in textbooks and workbooks.

From my students–all inservice teachers–I have gathered these suggestions. Some are so simple they may seem obvious, but often that is the place to begin.

• Select a short poem to read aloud each day–sometimes about the weather, sometimes funny, sometimes sad. Print the poem on a sheet of construction paper and post it in a prominent place where children can reread it easily.

• Invite children to help you choose a poem for the day and present it for class participation. This is a good time to repeat favorites heard earlier.

• Give the children frequent opportunities to become involved in impromptu choral reading–not to teach a lesson or analyze the poem, but to revel in the melody.

• From time to time, focus your selections on a theme: sports, people, weather, the moon and stars, or just plain fun. (A week of funny poems may be the pick-me-up everybody needs.)

• Have a week devoted to the work of one poet, such as John Ciardi or Aileen Fisher.

• Focus on poems related to an upcoming holiday.

• Help children select appropriate music to play as background while a poem is being read, or a song to sing softly as the setting for a poem. ("Kum-ba-ya" has proved to be just right for the poetry of Langston Hughes.)

• Show children how to improvise background music with rhythm instruments, water glasses, bells, or wooden sticks and blocks.

• Introduce body movement and improvised dance as often as possible with singing games, such as "Here We Go Looby-Lu" and "The Merry-Go-Round Song."

• Invite children to pantomime a poem as one child reads.

• Encourage children to stage an impromptu "poetry happening" with choral reading, music, song, and dance. This is a good way to spotlight poems they want to hear again.

Finding the Poems and Having Them Ready

The list of poetry books at the end of this chapter has a wealth of poems for all ages and occasions. I hope that each home and classroom can have a wide selection of these and similar books. As a beginning, have at least one general poetry anthology within easy reach. It should contain old poems and new, funny and serious, lyrics, limericks, ballads, and narrative.

Try to acquire several anthologies made up of poems about one particular subject or theme–poems about holidays or animals or farms.

As you extend your poetry shelf, try to get several collections by individual poets. This will help children recognize the body of work by one poet and begin to get the flavor of that person's poetry.

For many teachers, one of the great classroom aids is a card file of favorite poems–those you have and hope someday to introduce to children. If you group the poems by subject–pets, the sea, sports, and so on–both teacher and children will be able to make selections quickly. Perhaps children will offer to add their choices to yours. Some may want to start their own notebooks of favorite poems.

The tape recorder provides an inviting means of compiling a collection of children's favorite poems, with children reading their "poems too good to lose." In some classes, the tape recorder has become the impetus for better oral reading: "It's got to be right if it's on tape," children say, so they practice repeatedly before being entirely satisfied.

The possibilities are endless and very rewarding to all.

Reference

Sandburg, Carl. *Early moon.* New York: Harcourt Brace Jovanovich, 1930.

Children's Books

Brewton, John E. and Lorraine A. Blackburn., Editors. *They've Discovered a Head in the Box for the Bread and Other Laughable Limericks.* Illustrated by Fernando Krahn. Crowell, 1978.

Brewton, Sara, et al., Editors. *My Tang's Tungled and Other Ridiculous Situations.* Crowell, 1973.

Cole, Joanna, Editor. *A New Treasury of Children's Poetry: Old Favorites and New Discoveries.* Illustrated by Judith Gwyn Brown. Doubleday, 1984.

de Gasztold, Carmen Bernos. *Prayers from the Ark.* Viking, 1962.

Hubbell, Patricia. *The Apple Vendor's Fair.* Atheneum, 1963.

Hubbell, Patricia. *8 A.M. Shadows.* Atheneum, 1965.

Kuskin, Karla. *Dogs & Dragons, Trees & Dreams.* Harper and Row, 1980.

Larrick, Nancy, Editor. *Piping Down the Valleys Wild.* Dell, 1968.

Larrick, Nancy. *Tambourines! Tambourines to Glory! Prayers and Poems.* Atheneum, 1982.

Larrick, Nancy, Editor. *When the Dark Comes Dancing: A Bedtime Poetry Book.* Illustrated by John Wallner. Philomel, 1983.

Livingston, Myra Cohn. *A Song I Sang to You: A Selection of Poems.* Illustrated by Margot Tomes. Harcourt Brace Jovanovich, 1984.

McCord, David. *One at a Time.* Illustrated by Henry B. Kane. Little, Brown, 1977.

Merriam, Eve. *Out Loud.* Atheneum, 1973.

Moore, Lilian. *Something New Begins.* Illustrated by Mary Jane Dunton. Atheneum, 1982.

Silverstein, Shel. *A Light in the Attic.* Harper and Row, 1981.

Silverstein, Shel. *Where the Sidewalk Ends.* Harper and Row, 1974.

Wilner, Isabel, Editor. *The Poetry Troupe: Poems to Read Aloud.* Scribner, 1977.

Additional Children's Poetry Books

- Books by Individual Poets

Behn, Harry. *Crickets and Bullfrogs and Whispers of Thunder: Poems and Pictures by Harry Behn.* Edited by Lee Bennett Hopkins. Harcourt Brace Jovanovich, 1984.

Bodecker, N.M. *Hurry, Hurry, Mary Dear! and Other Nonsense Poems.* Atheneum, 1976.

Bodecker, N.M. *Let's Marry Said the Cherry and Other Nonsense Poems.* Atheneum, 1974.

Brooks, Gwendolyn. *Bronzeville Boys and Girls.* Illustrated by Ronni Solbert. Harper and Row, 1956.

Ciardi, John. *You Read to Me, I'll Read to You.* Illustrated by Edward Gorey. Lippincott, 1961.

Clifton, Lucille. *Everett Anderson's 1-2-3.* Illustrated by Ann Grifalconi. Holt, Rinehart and Winston, 1977.

Fisher, Aileen. *Listen, Rabbit.* Illustrated by Gail Owens. Crowell, 1964.

Fisher, Aileen. *Out in the Dark and the Daylight.* Harper and Row, 1980.

Frost, Robert. *A Swinger of Birches: Poems of Robert Frost for Young People.* Stemmer House, 1982.

Frost, Robert. *You Come Too.* Illustrated by Thomas W. Nason. Holt, Rinehart and Winston, 1959.

Giovanni, Nikki. *Spin a Soft Black Song.* Illustrated by Charles Bible. Hill and Wang, 1971.

Greenfield, Eloise. *Honey, I Love and Other Love Poems.* Illustrated by Diane and Leo Dillon. Crowell, 1978.

Holman, Felice. *At the Top of My Voice and Other Poems.* Illustrated by Edward Gorey. Scribner, 1970.

Holman, Felice. *The Song in My Head.* Illustrated by Jim Spanfeller. Scribner, 1985.

Kennedy, X.J. *The Forgetful Wishing Well: Poems for Young People.* Illustrated by Monica Incisa. Atheneum/McElderry, 1985.

Kennedy, X.J. *The Phantom Ice Cream Man: More Nonsense Verse.* Illustrated by David McPhail. Atheneum/McElderry, 1979.

Kuskin, Karla. *Near the Window Tree: Poems and Notes.* Harper and Row, 1975.

Livingston, Myra Cohn. *Celebrations.* Illustrated by Leonard Everett Fisher. Holiday House, 1985.

Lobel, Arnold. *The Book of Pigericks.* Harper and Row, 1983.

McCord, David. *Every Time I Climb a Tree.* Illustrated by Marc Simont. Little, Brown, 1967.

McCord, David. *One at a Time.* Illustrated by Henry B. Kane. Little, Brown, 1977.

Merriam, Eve. *Jamboree: Rhymes for All Times.* Illustrated by Walter Gaffney-Kessell. Dell, 1984.

Merriam, Eve. *Rainbow Writing.* Atheneum, 1976.

Moore, Lilian. *Something New Begins.* Illustrated by Mary Jane Dunton. Atheneum, 1982.

O'Neill, Mary. *Hailstones and Halibut Bones.* Illustrated by Leonard Weisgard. Doubleday, 1961.

Prelutsky, Jack. *The Headless Horseman Rides Tonight.* Illustrated by Arnold Lobel. Greenwillow, 1980.

Sandburg, Carl. *Early Moon.* Illustrated by James Daugherty. Harcourt Brace Jovanovich, 1930.

Sandburg, Carl. *Rainbows Are Made.* Compiled by Lee Bennett Hopkins. Illustrated by Fritz Eichenberg. Harcourt Brace Jovanovich, 1982.

Watson, Clyde. *Catch Me & Kiss Me & Say It Again.* Illustrated by Wendy Watson. Philomel, 1971.

Watson, Clyde. *Father Fox's Pennyrhymes.* Illustrated by Wendy Watson. Crowell, 1971.

Worth, Valerie. *Small Poems.* Illustrated by Natalie Babbitt. Farrar, Straus and Giroux, 1972.

Worth, Valerie. *Still More Small Poems.* Illustrated by Natalie Babbitt. Farrar, Straus and Giroux, 1978.

- Anthologies of Poems

Adams, Adrienne, Editor and Illustrator. *Poetry of Earth.* Scribner, 1972.

Amon, Aline, Editor and Illustrator. *The Earth Is Sore: Native Americans on Nature.* Atheneum, 1981.

Cole, William, Editor. *An Arkful of Animals: Poems for the Very Young.* Illustrated by Lynn Munsinger. Houghton Mifflin, 1978.

Cole, William, Editor. *Oh Such Foolishness!* Illustrated by Tomie dePaola. Lippincott, 1978.

Cole, William, Editor. *Poem Stew.* Illustrated by Karen Weinhaus. Lippincott, 1981.

Dunning, Stephen et al., Editors. *Reflections on a Gift of Watermelon Pickle and Other Modern Verse.* Lothrop, Lee and Shepard, 1966.

Engvick, William, Editor. *Lullabies and Night Songs.* Illustrated by Maurice Sendak. Harper and Row, 1965.

Fleming, Alice, Editor. *America Is Not All Traffic Lights: Poems of the Midwest.* Little, Brown, 1976.

Frank, Josette, Editor. *Poems to Read to the Very Young.* Random House, 1961.

Hopkins, Lee Bennett, Editor. *Moments: Poems about the Seasons.* Illustrated by Michael Hague. Harcourt Brace Jovanovich, 1980.

Hopkins, Lee Bennett, Editor. *A Song in Stone: City Poems.* Photographs by Anna Held Audette. Crowell, 1983.

Kennedy, X.J., and Dorothy M. Kennedy, authors and editors. *Knock at a Star: A Child's Introduction to Poetry.* Illustrated by Karen Ann Weinhaus. Little, Brown, 1982.

Larrick, Nancy, Editor. *On City Streets.* M. Evans, 1968.

Livingston, Myra Cohn, Editor. *Thanksgiving Poems.* Illustrated by Stephen Gammell. Holiday House, 1985.

Prelutsky, Jack, Editor. *Random House Book of Poetry for Children.* Illustrated by Arnold Lobel. Random House, 1983.

Yolen, Jane, Editor. *The Lullaby Song Book.* Illustrated by Charles Mikolaycak. Harcourt Brace Jovanovich, 1986.

Section 2
Children's Literature in the Primary Grades

For most children, reading begins in the primary grades (K through 3). Charlotte Huck and Kristen Kerstetter describe their approach to teaching developing readers in kindergarten. They stress the importance of creating a positive environment, reading aloud, and immersing children in literature from the very beginning. They recommend shared reading and shared writing and show how both are integrated with literature through the concept of webbing. Linda Lamme describes a whole language approach for teaching reading and the language arts. She establishes criteria for selecting books for a primary grade reading program; the best books at this level are repetitive, sequential, and predictable.

In this section as well as Sections 3 and 4, you will find specific teaching ideas by Lee Galda developed to promote higher level thinking. Galda illustrates strategies for helping students compare across books or for reading closely within books.

Chapter 4
Developing Readers

Charlotte S. Huck
Kristen Jeffers Kerstetter *

"My kindergarten class spent several days preparing for a field trip to a park. Once there, we divided into groups of five children with one adult, each group pursuing topics such as water, tracks, and shadows. As my group crossed over a wooden bridge, five boys began walking in unison shouting, 'TRIP TRAP TRIP TRAP!' Six-year-old Steve in his deepest, meanest, loudest voice bellowed, 'WHO'S THAT WALKING ON MY BRIDGE?' We quickly abandoned our topic and began playing with the idea of *The Three Billy Goats Gruff* (Asbjornsen and Moe). We told the story to one another, acted it out, and chanted the refrain as others crossed the bridge."

Children sometimes make connections between books and real life experiences in unexpected and exciting ways. How did Steve get to the point where bridge crossings could call up a literature experience? Obviously, Kristen's children were linking real life experiences with books they had heard read aloud at home or in school. Stories were giv-ing added meaning to their lives. As a sensitive teacher who values literature, Kristen was quick to seize the moment to extend and deepen their joy in literature.

Creating the Literacy Environment

If we want children to learn to read and to take delight in reading, we need to make their classroom environments as rich in literacy events as is Kristen's kindergarten. Children need to see a reason for reading and find personal meanings in stories. They need to be immersed in literature; surrounded by books, art, and writing materials of all kinds for extending and interpreting books; and given time to listen to and read stories.

Television and other media are so pervasive in our society that many children begin

---

* Note: The first person voice in this article is that of Kristen Kerstetter, a kindergarten teacher at Highland Park School in the Southwestern City School District in Grove City, Ohio.

school never having heard a story or having seen a significant adult in their lives reading a book. In order to counteract this neglect, schools need to become centers of rich literacy experiences. Listen to how Kristen creates such an environment.

"Just as parents play peekaboo and patty-cake in the same prescribed frame, they also all respond to their child's question 'But when will I learn to read?' with the same answer: 'When you go to school!' If children think this will happen the first day of kindergarten, I try to put books in their hands so they can read from the very start.

"Our classroom collection of some 400 titles is carefully selected and maintained throughout the year. Young children may be confused and intimidated by an entire library collection; they need to have a small enough choice to be able to find old favorites but also to discover new titles. Our PTA gives each teacher $300 a year to purchase books, we have a school media center from which we can draw books, and I use the public library. About once a month I change the collection, replenishing about one-fourth of the books with titles from the public library.

"When I'm ready to make a trip to the library, I post a sheet of paper and ask children to list books or subjects they want books about. When the new books arrive, I sit down with the children and pull the books out one at a time, telling something about each book, sharing a favorite picture or passage, or announcing that I've found a very special turtle book for Kelly because of his interest.

"I ask children to take on the responsibility for organizing the collection and allow them to create their own categories for books. This enables them to think about how books are related. If we are looking at counting books or ABC books, they will be grouped together. When we study the work of a particular author or illustrator like Ezra Jack Keats, all his books will be placed together. Children develop their own childlike categories, also. I remember one group made special groupings of baby books and spaghetti books, based on the size of the book; baby books were tiny while spaghetti books were tall and thin!

"Any book I read aloud is featured in a special place in the room so children can find it quickly and reread it–something they always want to do."

Reading Aloud

In his longitudinal study of the literacy achievement of children, Gordon Wells (1986) places much emphasis on the value of reading aloud. He talks about Jonathan, who ranked highest of all the children studied at seven and at the end of his schooling, and Rosie, who was at the bottom and never changed rank. Wells estimated that Jonathan had heard approximately 6,000 stories *before* entering school, while Rosie had not heard one.

Wells attributes much significance to the power of young children hearing stories read aloud. He focused on four activities he thought might account for children's differences in reading ability and found that only one, "listening to stories," was significantly related to the acquisition of literacy and later to reading comprehension at age seven.

This research is substantiated by other studies showing the importance of reading aloud to the development of readers. Thorndike's study (1973) of reading in fifteen countries showed that children who came from homes that respected reading and who had been read to from an early age were the best readers. Clark's study (1976) of young, fluent readers confirmed these findings in relation to children who had learned to read before they came to school. And Butler's account (1980) of books in the life of a multihandicapped girl provides a moving testament to the power of books in one child's life.

Dorothy Cohen's study (1968) suggests that if children have not been exposed to stories at home, it is not too late to do it in school. She initiated a year long read aloud project with second graders in New York City, including ten experimental and ten control classrooms. Cohen sent a list of books to the experimental teachers and asked them to read aloud every day for at least twenty minutes. She also asked them to do something with those books to make them significant.

The children could dramatize them, paint a picture of a favorite scene, compare one story with another–anything to make the story memorable. At the end of the year, the experimental group was significantly ahead of the control group in reading comprehension and reading vocabulary. Reading to children had helped the children learn to read. This study was later replicated by Cullinan, Jaggar, and Strickland (1974) in kindergarten through grade three, with similar results. It is obvious from her classroom practice that Kristen is aware of this research.

"I read to my children a lot–a whole lot. I read from one to three stories at a time. Sometimes I reread a favorite story twice. And I read two and three times a day–to the whole group, to small groups of four or five, and to individuals. I reread stories, just the way

Illustration from **The Doorbell Rang** by Pat Hutchins. Copyright © 1986 by Pat Hutchins. Greenwillow Books, a division of William Morrow and Company, Inc. Reprinted by permission.

children hear bedtime stories. It is not unusual for me to read a book twenty times in one month!

"When I read aloud, my objective is to make reading pleasurable and instructive. If I sit on a low chair, all of the children can see me when they sit on the rug. We might begin by looking at the cover of a book, say *The Doorbell Rang* by Pat Hutchins, and predict what the story might be from the picture and the title. Or I hold up the book and ask what other books they know by this author/illustrator. Some days I tell them to look for specific things and we discuss each page in detail. With some stories, such as *The Doorbell Rang,* I may stop before the last page and ask the children to guess what will happen. If it is another child at the door, will there be enough cookies to share? What will they do? Who else might it be? And then we read about the arrival of grandmother and her extra batch of cookies with real relief and joy. Sometimes I go back and reread the story, for one reading is seldom enough time to deal with a book on several levels. Some days I read two variations of a story and we discuss the differences, for example, between Oxenbury's "Henny-Penny" and Ormerod's *The Story of Chicken Licken.* We almost always talk about how a story could be extended in the class with art, drama, blocks, cooking, or reading other books and poems. Children are taught from the beginning that books can become the content for their work at school.

"Sometime each day I read two types of books: (1) those containing rich language, exciting plots, and beautiful pictures to stretch children's imaginations (such as books by Hutchins, Tomie dePaola, and William Steig, plus folktales and poetry) and (2) easy books children read along with me (I try to have multi-ple copies available). This category includes books with patterned texts such as *Brown Bear, Brown Bear* (Martin) or books from the Story Box by the Wright Group. These are the books children can take home after a few days, show their parents, and say 'Now I can read!'"

Shared Reading

Much of the way Kristen describes reading to children is what Don Holdaway (cited in Park, 1982) has called "shared reading." Holdaway observed parents interacting with their children when they read a book–talking about pictures and text, having the child find particular objects or words. He suggested the creation of "Big Books"–books with large type and illustrations–so a group of children could see the text and interact with it in the same way a parent and child share a book. Recommending the use of predictable books with patterned texts such as *The Very Hungry Caterpillar* (Carle), *Brown Bear, Brown Bear* (Martin), and *The Chick and the Duckling* (Ginsburg), children first hear the teacher read the story aloud from a regular sized book. Later, the teacher will use the big book and ask children to join in on the words they know or chant the refrains. Another time the teacher rereads the book, working on the development of concepts of print such as directionality or concepts of words and letters; hearing sounds in words; or finding specific words and framing them with their hands. Book handling techniques like turning pages, looking at the left page before the right page, and matching text with pictures are also emphasized. Children learn strategies for figuring out new words, such as using the meaning of the sentence, the structure of the word, guessing,

*Illustration from **The Teeny-Tiny Woman** by Paul Galdone. Copyright © 1984 by Paul Galdone. Reprinted by permission of Clarion Books/Ticknor & Fields, a Houghton Mifflin Company.*

reading on and coming back to look at a picture, or asking a friend. In the process of sharing the big book with children, the teacher demonstrates effective strategies for reading. The book will be read many times not only by the teacher but by children reading in twos or threes until they know the book by heart. This self-directed practice increases children's fluency and self-confidence. Gradually, as children practice acting like readers, they become readers.

"Once children know a text well, we may alter it or adapt it in a new way. 'Brown Bear, brown bear what do you see? I see a redbird looking at me' might become 'Papa bear, papa bear what do you see? I see a mama bear looking at me.' Baby bear and Goldilocks complete the chant. *The Teeny-Tiny Woman* (Galdone) is loved because of the repetition and scary elements. We tried to re-tell the story by making a counting chant and

illustrating each number with 'teeny tiny' pictures.

> One teeny tiny woman
> Two teeny tiny houses
> Three teeny tiny tombstones
> Four teeny tiny bones
> Five teeny tiny blankets
> Six teeny tiny shakes
> Seven teeny tiny yells
> Eight teeny tiny rolls
> Nine teeny tiny chatters
> Ten–TAKE IT!
> And all was quiet.

"Some books provide new formats that can be adapted for making big books. Eric Hill's lift-the-flap book *Nursery Rhymes* (Peek-a-Book) gives children the opportunity to play with different Mother Goose rhymes by asking other riddles, such as "Who lived in a shoe?" or "What did Mary grow?" Children can write the answers in the form of the verse on a lift-

Huck and Kerstetter

up-flap. An I Spy game with familiar book characters, found in *Each Peach Pear Plum* (Ahlberg and Ahlberg), could also serve as a model format.

Shared Writing

A natural outgrowth from shared reading is what Moira McKenzie (1985) has called "shared writing." Here the teacher acts as a scribe and writes stories, poems, or informational text as a group of children dictate them. Writing on a large sheet of newsprint, the teacher plays a key role in determining the pattern or shape of the text. As each sentence or section of the text is created by the children, the teacher explains what she is doing as she writes. She rereads the text many times, asking what idea should come next, questioning whether the story is making sense. Or she may talk about where to begin a sentence, the necessity for a capital letter, the need for space between words, or how various words are spelled. This shared writing helps children learn to write naturally, the same way shared reading helps children learn to read and enjoy it. Frank Smith (1982) says that for children to want to learn to write they must observe writing being done and see what it can do.

The techniques of shared writing can be used with a wide range of writing, including stories, alternative texts for well-known books, retelling stories, personal experiences, letters, recipes, verses, and songs. Teachers need to know the purpose for the writing in order to direct the text. If, for example, the primary purpose will be for shared reading, then they will ask questions that help generate predictable patterned writing, such as Kristen's text based on *The Teeny-Tiny Woman.* Such a story can be illustrated by the children and made into their own Big Book. If the purpose is to help children compose an imaginative story, the emphasis will be more on the development of plot and characters. One group of first graders who had had little exposure to books experienced difficulty in composing a story that had a real story line. Their teacher read them quantities of folktales such as *Little Red Riding Hood* (Grimm), *The Story of Three Little Pigs* (Jacobs), and *The Sleeping Beauty* (Grimm). Children then decided to compose their own story with the title of *Spot the King,* combining their love for Eric Hill's *Where's Spot?* with their new knowledge of folklore. Their story reflected the language of folktales, including such hyperbole as "He was the kindest king." and "He lived in the beautifuliest castle." Spot the King was killed by the dragon but awakened by a kiss from his Queen, surely a reflection of the children's hearing of *The Sleeping Beauty.* After the story was recorded it was made into a big book with the children's illustrations. Even though it was a long story, the children could read it easily because they had composed it and illustrated it.

Use of Reading and Writing in the Classroom

In *The Making of a Reader,* Marilyn Cochran-Smith (1984) differentiates between literacy events that occur during "rug-time," when books are shared more formally, and those literacy events when children use books and writing for their own purposes. In Kristen's room, daily work may revolve around a theme, and frequently that theme is related to books.

"One theme we used was a unit on 'Giants.' Children loved it. I prepared for it by brainstorming ideas and placing them on a web. Then I made a flow chart and decided what 'big events' would happen. Next I found books to support the study and brought in the thirty best titles I could find. Finally, I thought about what order to share the books–which books best supported one another? What characters were alike or different?

"*Fin M'Coul, The Giant of Knockmany Hill* (dePaola) was a good way to begin. First we made a list of everything the children said they knew about giants, then we tried to decide what kind of giant Fin was by examining the book cover. Fin is not unlike Big Anthony in dePaola's story of *Strega Nona*. Fin is not very bright, but he is very funny. His wife Oongh is clever and solves problems, just as Strega Nona does. We discussed similarities in these

Size relationships

Giants in school
  Biggest person in school
  Smallest child in school
Size relationships in pictures
  The King's Flower (Anno)
Make a giant cake
  Write and illustrate recipe
  Cook discusses recipes for
    feeding whole school
Compare giants and fairies
  *Imps, Demons, Hobgoblins,
    Witches, Fairies, and
    Elves* (Baskin)
  Record giant sounds and
    fairy sounds
  Find giant music and fairy
    music

Giant stories

Fin M'Coul (dePaola)
Giant John (Lobel)
Paul Bunyan (Kellogg)
Harald and the Giant Knight
  (Carrick)
Jim and the Beanstalk (Briggs)
Watch Out! A Giant (Carle)
*Monsters, Ghoulies and
  Creepy Creatures* (Hopkins)

Telling giant stories

Take a walk and look for signs
  of giants
Tell a giant story about
  creation of a playground, for
  example
Take a walk on a foggy day
  and look for dragon eggs
Develop charms for wishes and
  protection

Dramatize stories

The Great Big Enormous Turnip
  (Tolstoy)
Jack and the Beanstalk
  (Cauley)
Create puppets

Making giants

Make huge parts of a
  figure–head, arms, legs–join
  for huge giant
Make giant shadow on
  playground
  Runaway Giant (Holl)
Create huge beanstalk
  Jack and the Bean Tree
  (Haley)
Create stuffed giant family

GIANTS*

Giants of the past

Dragons
Saint George and the Dragon
  (Hodges)
Dinosaurs
If the Dinosaurs Came Back
  (Most)

Giants today

Skyscrapers
Football stadium
Airplanes
Machines
  *Mike Mulligan and His
    Steam Shovel* (Burton)
  Construction Giants (Olney)

*Adapted from *The Web*, pp. 14-15.

Huck and Kerstetter

two characters and were amazed at how alike they were.

"Our daily work centered around the study of giants. Four girls worked for a week making a giant family and writing about their experiences. Three other children made a puppet show about giants. One day we made a giant cake and speculated how much cake a giant could really eat. One of the children wrote about the cake:

This is a giant cake. The kids are eating it. A giant is going to eat the kids. I hope they don't get eaten. If they do I'll cry. Wah! Wah!
Jamie, age 5

"This was followed by a discussion with our school cook about the giant proportions needed to feed our student body."

Reading, writing, discussing, creating, thinking—all of these processes went on every day through the children's exploration of giants. Kristen did not give the children a worksheet asking them to color in a giant; they were busy creating their own huge ones from all sorts of materials. These worthwhile activities can substitute for the tremendous amount of time devoted to worksheets and workbooks that characterize so many of our classrooms today. *Becoming a Nation of Readers* (Anderson et al., 1985) decries our overreliance on workbooks and worksheets, maintaining that 70 percent of children's entire reading instruction is devoted to this kind of activity that is totally unrelated to year by year gains in reading proficiency. There is no doubt that Kristen's children were involved in real literacy events as they were immersed in their study of giants. They were becoming readers and enjoying the process.

Developing a Community of Readers

Susan Hepler (1982) speaks of a "community of readers." Children have to see their friends, older students, and teachers being really enthusiastic about books and reading if they are to become readers. If children never see their families reading, the schools will have to serve as models. Highland Park School is one example of a school that has made the development of readers their major priority.

"Our entire staff is devoted to using books as the core of our curriculum; we work hard to create a community of readers. Younger children have an opportunity to see older students reading for enjoyment for long periods of time. Older students frequently visit us to read a story to one or two children. Our children also visit other classes to read a story or to have one read to them. They also share the stories they have written and illustrated. Sometimes children draw three lines on the last page of a story they have written. After sharing the story with an adult or another student, this person records his or her name and writes a few comments, instilling a sense of pride and enjoyment in the author.

"The most exciting all school project that we have is the visit of an author/illustrator. Pat Hutchins was one such author. Profits from selling old textbooks and a book fair helped to finance her visit. It is essential to get books by the author into the hands of the children. Children bought hundreds of Hutchins's books at the book fair and we raided the public libraries, so we had many copies of her titles. The following activities are representative of this whole school study.

• On character day, every student and staff member dressed as a favorite Pat Hutchins character. Prizes were given for best swagger, longest mustache, and fluffiest features. Examples of prizes included a bag of wheat (*Rosie's Walk*), rolled up newspaper (*The Wind Blew*), and birthday hats (*Happy Birthday, Sam*).

• The school staff put on a play based on the book *One Eyed Jake.*

• The school lobby was transformed into a museum with significant objects and phrases from Hutchins's books prominently displayed. Rosie's footprints "walked" over the counter in the lobby.

• Schoolwide sustained reading was held one day with every child and adult reading a Pat Hutchins book at the same time. A sustained writing period followed the staff play.

• The book *Happy Birthday, Sam* portrays grandparents as thoughtful, loving people. The school had a Grandparents' Day to honor grandmas and grandpas. Each visitor received a favor representing a Pat Hutchins book.

• A schoolwide birthday party was preceded by the creation of a giant cake. Each class added certain ingredients, such as 25 eggs, and then passed the mixing bowl on to another class until the cake was completed. The giant cake was served at a whole school birthday party, complete with hats and favors made by the children.

"On the day of Pat Hutchins's visit the children were exploding with ideas and questions. The walls and tables were covered with books. Pat Hutchins spent the morning traveling from one class to another to view the displays and talk with the children. She ate lunch in the cafeteria, met with small groups, talked at an assembly, and autographed books.

"For one period each year all students and staff work together on one study. The oldest children are able to work on the same book young children are using. All of our energies are focused on one theme. What an exciting way to make authors seem like real people to children and to create a community of readers!"

Evaluation

Reading and writing skills are taught in Highland Park School, but they are always taught in the context of children's own purposes for reading and writing. Teachers are constantly evaluating children in this process oriented school. Kristen identifies some specific techniques used to evaluate students:

"Like most schools, we are required to use grade cards. Since these are not always reflective of our staff's philosophy, we have developed a language arts report that focuses on those areas we do value. We use the following questions to guide our writing of these reports:

• Do the children enjoy reading?

• Do they choose appropriate books?

• Do they use multiple strategies for figuring out new words?

• Do they proofread work?

• Do they choose to read at home?

"In addition to taking notes on my daily observation of children, I use several checklists to record where they are at the moment in reading. The checklists include:

• Shares books children can read

• Concepts of print test

• Letter/sound identification in context

• Tracking what books children read during the day

• Listening to children read individually

"We keep a language arts cumulative folder of children's writing from kindergarten on through school. These materials are dated and frequently shared with children and their parents to document growth.

"Hundreds of tests have been devised to tell teachers where children stand in reading at the end of kindergarten. But when Steve shouted "Who's that walking on my bridge?", I knew more about his reading acquisition than any standardized test could measure. That moment in the park was only one of many daily interactions that told me Steve was integrating books into his daily life. Reading for Steve is the continuation of his first five years of taking on a sense of story, finding pleasure in language, gathering book knowledge, and understanding print concepts. Reading should never be limited to a morning period of round robin reading of the same book and filling in blanks in workbooks. Reading should be a natural, everyday, all day occurrence. Books under bridges in parks? They are there if you will only look."

References

Anderson, Richard C. et al. *Becoming a nation of readers.* Washington: National Institute of Education, U.S. Department of Education, 1985.

Butler, Dorothy. *Cushla and her books.* Boston: The Horn Book, 1980.

Clark, Margaret. *Young fluent readers.* Portsmouth, NH: Heinemann, 1976.

Cochran-Smith, Marilyn. *The making of a reader.* Norwood, NJ: Ablex, 1984.

Cohen, Dorothy. The effect of literature on vocabulary and reading achievement. *Elementary English,* 1968, *45,* 209-213, 217.

Cullinan, Bernice E., Jaggar, Angela, and Strickland, Dorothy. Language expansion for black children in the primary grades: A research report. *Young Children,* 1974, *29,* 98-112.

Hepler, Susan Ingrid. *Patterns in response to literature: A one year study of a fifth and sixth grade classroom.* Unpublished doctoral dissertation, Ohio State University, 1982.

McKenzie, Moira. Shared writing. *Language matters.* London: Inner London Educational Authority, 1985.

Park, Barbara. The big book trend: A discussion with Don Holdaway. *Language Arts,* 1982, *59.*

Smith, Frank. *Writing and the writer.* New York: Holt, Rinehart and Winston, 1982.

Thorndike, Robert L. *Reading comprehension, education in 15 countries: An empirical study.* Vol. 3, International Studies in Education. New York: Holstead Wiley, 1973.

The Web, 1985, *9* (4), 14-15. (Center for Language, Literature, and Reading, College of Education, The Ohio State University, Columbus, Ohio.)

Wells, Gordon. *The meaning makers: Children learning language and using language to learn.* London: Heinemann, 1986.

Children's Books

Ahlberg, Janet, and Allen Ahlberg. *Each Peach Pear Plum.* Viking, 1978.

Anno, Mitsumasa. *The King's Flower.* Collins, 1979.

Asbjornsen, P.C., and J.E. Moe. *The Three Billy Goats Gruff.* Illustrated by Marcia Brown. Harcourt Brace Jovanovich, 1957.

Baskin, Leonard. *Imps, Demons, Hobgoblins, Witches, Fairies, and Elves.* Pantheon, 1983.

Briggs, Raymond. *Jim and the Beanstalk.* Coward, McCann and Geoghegan, 1970.

Burton, Virgina Lee. *Mike Mulligan and His Steam Shovel.* Houghton Mifflin, 1939.

Carle, Eric. *The Very Hungry Caterpillar.* Philomel, 1969.

Carle, Eric. *Watch Out! A Giant!* Collins World, 1978.

Carrick, Donald. *Harald and the Giant Knight.* Clarion, 1982.

Cauley, Lorinda Bryan. *Jack and the Beanstalk.* Putnam, 1983.

dePaola, Tomie. *Fin M'Coul, The Giant of Knockmany Hill.* Holiday House, 1981.

dePaola, Tomie. *Strega Nona.* Prentice-Hall, 1975.

Galdone, Paul. *The Teeny-Tiny Woman.* Houghton Mifflin, 1984.

Ginsburg, Mirra. *The Chick and the Duckling.* Illustrated by Jose Aruego and Ariane Aruego. Macmillan, 1972.

Grimm, Jacob, and Wilhelm Grimm. *Little Red Riding Hood.* Retold and illustrated by Trina Schart Hyman. Holiday House, 1983.

Grimm, Jacob, and Wilhelm Grimm. *The Sleeping Beauty.* Retold and illustrated by Warwick Hutton. Atheneum, 1979.

Haley, Gail E. *Jack and the Bean Tree.* Crown, 1986.

Hill, Eric. *Nursery Rhymes.* (Peek-a-Book.) Price/Stern/Sloan, 1982.

Hill, Eric. *Where's Spot?* G.P. Putnam's, 1980.

Hodges, Margaret (Adapter). *Saint George and the Dragon.* Illustrated by Trina Shart Hyman. Little, Brown, 1984.

Holl, Adelaide. *The Runaway Giant.* Illustrated by Mamoru Funai. Lothrop, Lee and Shepard, 1967.

Hopkins, Lee Bennett. *Monsters, Ghoulies, and Creepy Creatures.* Illustrated by Vera Rosenberry. Albert Whitman and Co., 1977.

Hutchins, Pat. *The Doorbell Rang.* Greenwillow, 1986.

Hutchins, Pat. *Happy Birthday, Sam.* Greenwillow, 1978.

Hutchins, Pat. *One Eyed Jake.* Greenwillow, 1979.

Hutchins, Pat. *Rosie's Walk.* Macmillan, 1968.

Hutchins, Pat. *The Wind Blew.* Macmillan, 1974.

Jacobs, Joseph. *The Story of the Three Little Pigs.* Illustrated by Lorinda Bryan Cauley. G.P. Putnam's Sons, 1980.

Kellogg, Steven. *Paul Bunyan.* William Morrow, 1984.

Lobel, Arnold. *Giant John.* Harper and Row, 1964.

Martin Bill Jr. *Brown Bear, Brown Bear, What Do You See?* Illustrated by Eric Carle. Holt, Rinehart and Winston, 1983.

Most, Bernard. *If the Dinosaurs Came Back.* Harcourt Brace Jovanovich, 1984.

Olney, Ross. *Construction Giants.* Atheneum, 1984.

Ormerod, Jan. *The Story of Chicken Licken.* Lothrop, Lee and Shepard, 1985.

Oxenbury, Helen. *The Helen Oxenbury Nursery Story Book.* Knopf, 1985.

Tolstoy, Alexei. *The Great Big Enormous Turnip.* Illustrated by Helen Oxenbury. Watts, 1969.

Wright Story Box Group. *In a Dark Dark Wood.* Selected by June Melsu and Joy Crowley. Wright Story Box Group, 1980.

Wright Story Box Group. *Mrs. Wishy-Washy.* Selected by Joy Crowley. Wright Story Box Group, 1980.

Chapter 5
Children's Literature: The Natural Way to Learn to Read

Linda Leonard Lamme

Tameshia was sitting on the school bus carefully pointing to each word in a book and singing, "Mary wore her red dress, red dress, red dress,..." The bus driver had to remind her to get off the bus and in doing so commented on her reading. Tameshia replied, "I learned to read on the first day of school! Wait till Ma sees this!"

Tameshia had indeed learned a lot about reading that first day of school. First thing in the morning her teacher asked the children if they would like to sing some of their favorite songs. Tameshia suggested "Mary Wore Her Red Dress." After the class had sung the song, the teacher showed them *Mary Wore Her Red Dress and Henry Wore His Green Sneakers* (Peek). She sang/read the book with the children several times (at their request) pointing to each word. The last time they sang, the teacher tape recorded them. She then put the book in the listening center and showed the children how to run the tape recorder and use the earphones. The teacher noticed that Tameshia returned to the listening center several times during free play to listen to the tape and look at the book, so at the close of school she asked Tameshia if she would like to borrow the book for the night to read to her parents.

How different Tameshia's experience is from that of many children who spend their reading time in school filling out worksheets and reading stories from uninteresting books. Instead of coming home with a list of words to memorize or worksheets to correct, Tameshia comes home excited, entertains her parents, and receives accolades for her first steps toward becoming a reader.

Many primary school teachers recognize that children can be taught at school the way early readers are "taught" at home–by reading stories in real books. Right from the start the goal of reading instruction is to help children become avid readers, for if children love to read, they will read, and if they do read, they will become competent readers. However, many children who are drilled on reading skills never learn to love to read and never read anything beyond what is required. Individuals who can read but don't are no better off than individuals who cannot read. They might as well be illiterate, for they derive none of the pleasure or information from print that readers enjoy.

A key to developing early and successful primary school readers is to replicate as far as possible the conditions prevailing in the homes of early readers. How do most of these early readers achieve success so easily? Writing and pointing out environmental print have a lot to do with learning how to read (Sulzby, 1985). The core of a home reading program, however, is lap reading–the stories most early readers enjoy prior to naptime and bedtime every day prior to entering school. Children with this sort of background usually come to school loving books; they possess a storehouse of solid concepts about reading.

The way a child views reading is important. An ethnographic study revealed that first graders in the high and low reading groups have vastly different concepts about reading (Bondy, 1985). Children in the high reading group think reading is a way of learning, a private pleasure, and a social activity. In contrast, children in the low reading group think reading is saying the words correctly (or cracking the code), doing schoolwork, and a source of status. It is no wonder that the children in the low group have difficulty learning how to read. They don't even know what reading is all about.

Activities in the classroom contribute to children's concepts of reading. The methods and materials used by primary grade teachers have influence beyond what has traditionally been recognized in contributing to the ease with which children learn to read.

Whole Language Classroom Routines

A literature based reading program is rooted in the whole language approach, which has children learn from whole language units, such as songs, poems, and simple stories. Reading is done in context, as opposed to a basic skills approach in which children learn isolated skills such as letter sounds. The amount of transfer from skillpacks and worksheets to the actual process of reading is questionable. Letters and sounds are abstract concepts for children in the concrete operations stage of cognitive development.

Whole language approaches stem from research (Newman, 1985; Smith, 1981) on successful learners, especially early readers who learned how to read at home without school instruction. The methods of instruction aim at helping all children adopt the reading behaviors of good readers recognizing that there are some important distinctions between good and poor readers.

• When they come to an unfamiliar word, good readers use many different word analysis strategies, while poor readers "sound it out." If sounding it out fails, poor readers have no alternatives.

• Good readers self correct if they make

a mistake that does not make sense; poor readers ignore their reading errors.

- Good readers read for meaning; poor readers read to pronounce words correctly.

- Good readers reread favorite books and become fluent readers; poor readers seldom reread and thus rarely experience fluency.

- Good readers seek out books by favorite authors; poor readers don't notice who wrote the books they read.

- Good readers read for their own pleasure; poor readers read because it is a school assignment.

- Good readers discuss books with their friends and exchange opinions on good books to read; poor readers do not discuss reading.

The strategies teachers use to achieve positive reading behaviors are similar to those used in literate homes. They fit the strategies into a literature oriented reading program through a series of daily activities involving books.

Reading Aloud by the Teacher

Several times each day the teacher reads aloud for the entertainment of the children. It is amazing how many adults remember a teacher who read aloud to them in elementary school. We have forgotten the worksheets and textbooks, but we remember being read to. An activity that has such a lasting impact must be worth a great deal. While reading aloud, the teacher models reading behavior. Reading aloud also whets the appetite for good stories. It exposes children to literature they would not be able to read themselves. It shows them what real readers do and gives them a goal for learning to read.

If books that are read aloud are placed in the classroom reading collection, children can learn to read by rereading familiar books, just as children do at home. Reading aloud creates a community spirit surrounding books; it gives children something to talk about, a reference point for extending literature into the entire school day. Witness a first grade teacher who asked the children to line up

Big Books and Little Books

A kindergarten teacher made a "big book" of the children's favorite Mother Goose rhymes and another of modern rhymes. Big books (Holdaway, 1979) are used to replicate lap reading with small groups of children. They are exact copies of storybooks, but are large enough to be seen by a group of children.
- The teacher copied the words from her big books into two small replicas for each child in the class to take home.
- Parents were asked to read one of the books aloud to their child before bed each night. They were very enthusiastic about their children's emerging reading behaviors.

Adapted from an idea by Eileen Rudenko, Duval Elementary School, Gainesville, Florida.

Teaching Idea

Daily Reading

One first grade teacher has dealt with the problem of students not having time or a place to read at home. Each morning one of the seatwork assignments she gives the class is "Read a book."

Adapted from an idea by Sandra Kolb, Stephen Foster Elementary School, Gainesville, Florida.

right behind one another, "just like *Swimmy*" (Lionni).

Chanting from Charts

Primary school teachers have long used charts as part of their instructional programs. Language experience advocates take dictation from groups of children to make simple, repetitive charts that are easy to read. A chart on "Our Pets" might include this sentence pattern: "Laurel has a cat named Tosh." "Ary has a dog named Winn." "David has a hamster named Lew."

When these sentence patterns come directly from children's books, the literature connection is even stronger. Songs and chants found in children's books can be reproduced on charts for oral chanting or singing. New verses can be invented using the children's names for easy reading. "Sam, Sam, what do you see?" is easily recognized by children as a variant of *Brown Bear, Brown Bear* (Martin).

Using charts until the children can read what is on them is important. Many teachers find that beginning readers learn concepts of print by playing with written language as they played with oral language when learning how to talk. These teachers make duplicate copies of charts in the form of sentence strips that children can manipulate or match with the

print on charts. It is easier, of course, for children to match whole sentences or phrases than to match individual words. But as children become more accomplished at reading, they can put the words to familiar verses in the proper order by manipulating the words like a puzzle.

Silent Reading by Children

A very important part of the reading process is selecting something to read and sustaining silent reading long enough to get something out of the reading material (Sulzby, 1985). Many children never read anything that is not assigned by the teacher. They go to a library and are at a loss for how to find a good book to read. Many children come from homes where there is no quiet moment without television or some other activity, so they never have a quiet time set aside for reading. Silent reading needs to occur daily.

Lap Reading

For children just learning to read, there is no substitute for reading one-on-one with an accomplished reader. When we read aloud to groups there is less opportunity to be responsive to individuals, to have children turn

"Read Time" for the Whole School

One elementary school principal designates "Read Time" throughout her school.

- At the end of each day the children prepare to go home and then either the teacher reads aloud or the children read silently for the last twenty minutes of the day.
- This principal reports several unexpected results of her "Read Time" program.
  - The circulation in the school library has increased more than 40 percent, for each child has to have a book available to read at the end of the day.
  - "Read Time" creates a calm, pleasant mood, which is reflected in a substantial decrease in the number of altercations in bus lines and among children who walk home.

Adapted from an idea by Kathryn Eward, W.J. Creel Elementary School, Melbourne, Florida.

Teaching Idea

the pages, to follow the print with their eyes, and to make comments about what they are reading. Yet few teachers find they are able to spend fifteen minutes a day with each child who is learning to read. A solution is to invite volunteers such as senior citizens into the classroom to sit in a comfortable chair and read with individual children.

Book Discussions

Reading in a large group, with a buddy, or by oneself gives children reading time during the day, but to progress in reading ability, children need to put reading into a social context as well. Book discussions, held after a read aloud session or silent reading time, can be structured in many different ways.

Sometimes teachers meet with small groups while the rest of the class is reading. Then the teacher asks comprehension questions about character and plot, which get the children to think about and share what they are reading.

In one school all the kindergarten children take a book home each night for their parents or older siblings to read to them. Each day starts with sharing time where the children tell about what was read to them the night before; then they exchange books. Enlisting parental help is a sure way to help a literature reading program succeed.

Writing

Daily writing by primary children often reflects their daily reading. Some children keep reading journals or diaries with their reactions to the books they are reading.

Child illustrated books make another important addition to the classroom library. Many primary classrooms participate in Writer's Workshop where the children write and revise their work with the goal of publishing their pieces in handmade books.

Storytelling

Even before children read stories, they can tell them; such oral language activities lead into reading. Storytellers learn many concepts about reading, especially story sequence or schema, phrasing, and dialogue. Young children benefit from the concreteness of story enactment. By supplying a few simple props, teachers encourage children to act out familiar tales. Children enjoy telling puppet and flannelboard stories. Use of these manipulatives helps children, especially kinesthetic learners, remember storylines.

Storytelling without props, however, is an important experience for young children. In a study which examined the responses of preschoolers to told versus flannelboard stories, it was obvious the children attended more to the tale itself in the told version and to the visual characters in the flannelboard version. In addition, the children were more involved verbally and physically in the told version (Kaiser, 1985).

The Reading Materials

There are several kinds of books especially well suited for helping children learn to read. Books with the elements of prediction–repetition and sequence–are prime sources for beginning reading material (Rhodes, 1981). Some of these are produced as big books; for example, *A House Is a House for Me* (Hoberman), *Brown Bear, Brown Bear* (Martin), and *Mrs. Wishy-Washy* (Wright Story Box Program). Big books make it possible for every child to see the print as groups read them together.

Books labeled easy to read are often deceptive. Some are written in simplified language with short sentences and controlled vocabulary. This kind of writing may actually make a story less predictable and the language less natural than a story not written by formula. Many of these books are, therefore, more difficult to read than some regular children's picture books that are predictable and use precise vocabulary (Moe, 1978). Because controlled vocabulary books may lack the sophisticated language needed to make them enjoyable listening, they are best used for silent reading if children elect to read them.

There are several factors to consider when selecting books for a primary reading program. First, there should be variety–picture books, folklore, fantasy, and poetry–as each type of book has something special to offer the beginning reader. Second, the stories should deal with a range of real life and imaginative topics. Children need to see themselves in books, but they also need to stretch their imaginations. Books with these characteristics will be memorable and will invite rereading. Third, books of good quality need to form the core of the collection. The stories should have well developed characters, interesting language, engaging plots, and vivid themes. Although it is tempting to read aloud to the class any book a child brings from home, it is better for children to have the books that are read aloud represent the best of children's literature. You risk boring or frustrating children when you share with them books that are poorly written or illustrated.

How does a primary grade teacher go about acquiring quality children's books? Some teachers spend money they formerly spent on workbooks. Also, with help from parents and parent groups, it is not hard to stock a primary grade classroom with 400 or 500 children's books (many paperbacks), including multiple copies of favorites (Milz, 1985). The classroom also needs several subscriptions to

Older Child as Reader

Children of different ages can be paired for reading time. For example, fifth graders might read to kindergarteners or first graders.

- Every other Friday afternoon one kindergarten teacher goes to a fifth grade to train the older children in reading aloud to younger ones. Because scheduling does not permit all of the fifth graders to come to the kindergarten, each fifth grader reads to two kindergarten children at once.
- This teacher reports three key factors that insure a successful buddy reading program.
  - First, the program needs to be carefully planned so the children know precisely when and where to meet and what to do.
  - Second, the older children need training in how to read aloud from different types of books.
  - Third, book selection is critical. It is important to find books that the older children can read successfully to the younger ones and ones the younger children will enjoy.

Inevitably the children's comments are enthusiastic about buddy reading. One fourth grade boy was absent one day and missed reading with his kindergarten buddy. When the child returned to school the following day, he asked his teacher if his buddy had been read to, and when the teacher told him who had taken his place, the boy went right over to the substitute and asked how his buddy had done and "Did he behave himself?" This kind of responsible behavior was new for this particular boy.

Adapted from an idea by Suzanne Colvin, Duval Elementary School, and Josephine Reddick, Stephen Foster Elementary School, Gainesville, Florida.

Teaching Idea

high quality children's magazines for primary grades, such as *Highlights for Children, Ranger Rick's Nature Magazine,* and *Cricket.* Weston Woods and Scholastic are sources of audiovisual media on children's literature.

With these guidelines in mind, the following types of books are especially effective for helping primary grade children to become avid readers.

Books that Are Repetitive

We have all heard children ask to have the same story read repeatedly. Researchers looking at emergent reading behaviors have documented the value of repetitive readings for young children (Holdaway, 1979; Clay, 1985). Depending on the type of book being read, children are learning language patterns, story schemata, and sequence by hearing and reading books repeatedly. They eventually match the words they say with the words they see.

Chants, such as *Brown Bear, Brown Bear* (Martin) and song picture books such as *Oh A-Hunting We Will Go* (Langstaff) are so repetitive they can be read instantly. Young chil-

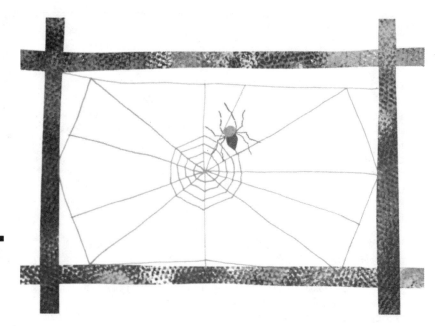

*Illustration by Eric Carle reprinted by permission of Philomel Books from **The Very Busy Spider** by Eric Carle, copyright © 1984 by Eric Carle.*

dren can easily repeat what goes with each picture, and since only a word or two change on each page the chant becomes easy to memorize. Similarly, children learn that there is a match between the chant they have memorized and the print on the page.

Several parts of a story can be repeated. Stories such as *The Little Red Hen* (Galdone) have repetitive phrases such as, " 'Not I,' said the...." throughout the story. In *The Doorbell Rang* (Hutchins), a highly repetitive and predictable book, the line " 'And no one makes cookies like Grandma,' said Ma as the doorbell rang." is repeated five times. The book also appeals because of its touch of humor and surprise ending.

Two sentences are repeated eight times in *The Very Busy Spider* (Carle). Each time another animal asked the spider to play, "The spider didn't answer. She was very busy spinning her web." The book is predictable because each animal makes its common animal sound and asks the spider to partici-

pate in an activity commonly associated with that animal, as in, " 'Oink, Oink,' grunted the pig. 'Want to roll in the mud?' " The sentence patterns repeat and there is great content predictability in this story.

Several stories have the text or a summary of it repeated at or near the end of the book for a review. *Good-Night, Owl!* (Hutchins) is an example. The entire text is repeated verbatim. In *Mr. Gumpy's Outing* (Burningham), passengers in the boat do just what Mr. Gumpy predicted they might do earlier in the book, which forms a summary of the action all on one page.

Cumulative stories combine a repetitive format with a new character or event to set the stage for prediction. In *Drummer Hoff* (Emberley) each officer contributes one more item toward the firing of the cannon, and each time the previous contributions are repeated right down to, "but Drummer Hoff fired it off." A well known cumulative rhyme is *The House that Jack Built* (Galdone). *Bringing*

Learning about Illustrators

In one first grade the entire class studies children's book illustrators.

- The teacher gathers all the books by a particular illustrator, reads them to the children, and has them on display for a week or longer.
- When the children finish studying these books, they participate in art projects using the media of the illustrator and write notes to the illustrator.
- The teacher binds these notes into a book and mails them to the illustrator, who typically responds by sending the class a letter, often including a photo or drawing. The responses are placed in a photo album and put in the classroom reading corner.

Adapted from an idea by Vera Milz, Way Elementary School, Bloomfield Hills, Michigan.

the Rain to Kapiti Plain (Aardema) is the same sort of rhythmic tale that tells how Kipat ingeniously brings rain to the arid Kapiti Plain. Each verse ends with

> The big, black cloud,
> all heavy with rain,
> that showered the ground
> on Kapiti Plain.

With cumulative tales it is fun to give each child or group of children different lines to recite until, at the end, the whole class is chanting the rhyme. Most, but not all, cumulative tales rhyme. In *One Fine Day* (Hogrogrian), the fox carries out the directions of an assortment of individuals in order to have his tail sewn back on. This tale is not a rhyme, but it does repeat all of the events in reverse order when the fox finally is able to meet the demands of his creditors.

Some stories have refrains. *Chicken Soup with Rice* (Sendak) contains a slight variation in each chorus of "Sipping once, sipping twice, sipping chicken soup with rice." Many songs that normally are sung with refrains do not have the refrains included in the book version, but these can be added if the words are written on charts or in homemade books.

Some folktales repeat segments of the plot three times. Examples are *The Three Billy Goats Gruff* (Blair), *The Three Bears* (Galdone) and *The Three Little Pigs* (Galdone). After the first and second animal have climbed over the bridge, sat in a chair, or built a house, children can anticipate what the third will do. Exposure to an ugly troll and a big bad wolf also builds children's concepts of the role of a villain in a folktale.

A final aspect of repetition comes when teachers read aloud and present in printed form (either books or charts) language that children already know, such as Mother Goose rhymes and songs. Teachers will want several comprehensive Mother Goose collections that have one rhyme on a page and large enough pictures to be seen by a group. *Brian Wildsmith's Mother Goose* and *Tomie de-*

Paola's Mother Goose are ideal. Teachers need to read aloud favorite stories, rhymes, and songs repeatedly. They might read two different versions of the same tale or song, such as *Fiddle-I-Fee* (Galdone; Stanley) and compare them.

Books that Are Sequential

Primary children typically have an elementary understanding of sequence. They can count by rote (even if they don't understand one to one correspondence), and they know the days of the week and some of the months of the year. Daily routines follow familiar sequences and can be part of realistic stories. Folktales have sequential plots that children quickly identify. Storybooks containing sequences familiar to children are easy to read because they are predictable.

In *The Very Hungry Caterpillar* (Carle), the caterpillar eats *one* apple on *Monday, two* pears on *Tuesday,* etc. The sequence of activities makes this book a sure success with a beginning reader.

Many songs are sequential and repetitive. *10 Bears in My Bed* (Mack) can be read easily after one hearing with the repetition, picture clues, and sequence from ten down to one. *Busy Monday Morning* (Domanska) contains both sequence and repetition of sentence pattern. An example is "On a Tuesday morning, busy Tuesday morning, Father raked the hay. We raked hay together he and I." The verses in some songs are sequential. In both *The Farmer in the Dell* (Zuromskis) and *London Bridge Is Falling Down* (Spier), each verse leads to the next.

Alphabet and counting books show another kind of sequence. Concept books, especially those containing environmental print, help children see the connection between reading books and words in their environment. Examples include *School Bus* (Crews), *Truck* (Crews), *Cars* (Rockwell). Tana Hoban specializes in illustrating simple concept books with beautiful photographs, such as *Big Ones, Little Ones* and *Is it Red? Is it Yellow? Is it Blue?*

A Peaceable Kingdom: The Shaker Abecedarius (Provensen) is an alphabetic rhyme sung to the tune of the "Alphabet Song." Each animal appears from left to right in both picture and word, with plenty of white space between words. Primary school children like books with challenging words (animals unfamiliar to them) that they can memorize easily because they are in song form. This book is outstanding for both word boundaries and left-right progression, as well as for an appreciation of Shaker culture.

The bedtime book *Ten, Nine, Eight* (Bang) involves counting backwards in rhymes accompanied by clear illustrations until we see "one big girl all ready for bed." In *I See* (Isadora) and *Noisy* (Hughes), the children end up in bed as well. In *Silly Goose* (Ormerod), a little girl says simple sentences like "I flap like a bat." to the accompaniment of an animal picture on each page.

Several cardboard books appeal to primary grade children while entertaining preschoolers as well. The First Look Nature Books (Hands) tell what little animals see. Baby Animal Board Books (Lilly) and a series by Random House that includes *Animal Swimmers* (Lilly) are two more examples of interesting science books.

Measuring Children's Progress

How can teachers keep track of children's progress without unit tests and graded worksheets? Alternatives include having children keep written records of each book they can read fluently or, if they are older, a brief summary of each book they have read. Children can write a paragraph about why they did or did not like a book.

Teachers can develop a checklist they fill out as they observe and listen to children read. An example follows of behaviors teachers might want to monitor (Lamme, 1985).

- Shows interest in words
- Can tell a familiar story
- Can make up a story
- Can point to individual words on a page
- Can turn the pages at the appropriate time when a story is being read aloud
- Can find a familiar book on a bookshelf
- Chooses to read or look at books during free time
- Notices words and symbols in the environment
- Spells words developmentally
- Chooses to write during free time
- Asks questions about print
- Paces dictation (dictates at a slow speed so someone can write down what the child is dictating)
- Is aware that print has meaning

Questions about Literature

One teacher has developed a literature unit using questions from all levels of Bloom's taxonomy for each of the stories in her collection. Children work in pairs to answer these thought questions.

Adapted from an idea by Margaret Broadbent, Fayetteville Elementary School, Fayetteville, New York.

Teaching Idea

Sharing Literature

In one third grade the children have "Literature Share Time."
- Each child selects a page or two from a book he or she has recently finished to read aloud to a group of two or three children.
- After a child has read a selection, there is a short time for comments and questions about the book from the audience.
- The children keep a written record of the titles of the books they have shared.

Adapted from an idea by Betsy Nies, Gainesville Country Day School, Gainesville, Florida.

Teaching Idea

A Month of Stories

One second grade teacher put aside the regular reading materials for a month of storytelling in the classroom.

- Each child selected a story to learn and took the book home to have his or her parents read aloud for a week.
- By the end of the month, the teacher had videotaped each child in the room telling a story to a group of kindergarteners. It was especially heartwarming to see some of the poorer readers in the class take center stage and proudly spin a tale to the entertainment of an audience.
- The children returned to their reading instruction with a far more comprehensive view of what stories are all about.

Adapted from an idea by Donna Sides, Prairie View Elementary School, Gainesville, Florida.

- Remembers details from stories
- Predicts outcomes in stories
- Compares books, authors, or illustrators
- Has favorite books
- Borrows books from the library
- Rereads favorite books
- Stops reading books he or she does not like after looking at a few pages
- Uses books as resources for school reports
- Brings to school books on topics the class is studying
- Comments about books read

Finally, several standardized book awareness measures, such as the *Concepts about Print Test* (Clay, 1985), can be administered individually to children.

Most parents won't need test results or checklists to prove that their children are making progress. If teachers give pointers in newsletters or workshops, parents understand that progress is not measured by the number of worksheets their children bring home, but by their children's enthusiasm for reading and the amount of reading they choose to do independently. A child who is an avid and enthusiastic reader by the end of third grade will be a reader for life. There is no doubt the avid reader will continue to develop competence in the upper elementary grades. Just as with so many other activities in life, the more time children put into practicing their skills, the more talented they become at that activity. Enthusiastic readers become talented readers.

References

Bondy, Elizabeth. Classroom influences on children's conceptions of reading. Paper delivered at National Association of Education of Young Children Conference, New Orleans, 1985.

Clay, Marie. *The early detection of reading difficulties,* third edition. Portsmouth, NH: Heinemann, 1985.

Holdaway, Don. *The foundations of literacy.* Portsmouth, NH: Heinemann, 1979.

Kaiser, Amy. *Preschool children's responses to two styles of storytelling.* Master's thesis, University of Florida, 1985.

Lamme, Linda Leonard. *Growing up reading.* Washington: Acropolis Books, 1985.

Milz, Vera. First graders' uses for writing. In Angela M. Jaggar and M. Trika Smith-Burke (Eds.), *Observing the language learner.* Newark, DE: International Reading Association, 1985.

Moe, Alden J. Using picture books for reading vocabulary development. In John Warren Stewig and Sam Leaton Sebesta (Eds.), *Using literature in the classroom.* Urbana, IL: National Council of Teachers of English, 1978.

Newman, Judith M. (Ed.). *Whole language: Theory in use.* Portsmouth, NH: Heinemann, 1985.

Rhodes, Lynn K. I can read! Predictable books as resources for reading and writing instruction. *The Reading Teacher,* 1981, *34,* 511-518.

Smith, Frank. Demonstrations, engagements, and sensitivity: A revised approach to language learning. *Language Arts,* 1981, *58,* 1, 103-112.

Sulzby, Elizabeth. Children's emergent reading of favorite storybooks: A developmental study. *Reading Research Quarterly,* 1985, *20,* 4, 459-481.

Children's Books

Aardema, Verna. *Bringing the Rain to Kapiti Plain.* Illustrated by Beatriz Vidal. Dial, 1981.

Bang, Molly. *Ten, Nine, Eight.* Greenwillow, 1983.

Blair, Susan. *The Three Billy-Goats Gruff.* Scholastic, 1974.

Burningham, John. *Mr. Gumpy's Outing.* Holt, Rinehart and Winston, 1970.

Carle, Eric. *The Very Busy Spider.* Philomel, 1985.

Carle, Eric. *The Very Hungry Caterpillar.* Philomel, 1969.

Crews, Donald. *School Bus.* Greenwillow, 1984.

Crews, Donald. *Truck.* Greenwillow, 1980.

dePaola, Tomie. *Tomie dePaola's Mother Goose.* Putnam, 1985.

Domanska, Janina. *Busy Monday Morning.* Greenwillow, 1985.

Emberley, Barbara. *Drummer Hoff.* Illustrated by Ed Emberley. Prentice-Hall, 1967.

Galdone, Paul. *Cat Goes Fiddle-I-Fee.* Clarion, 1985.

Galdone, Paul. *The House that Jack Built.* McGraw-Hill, 1961.

Galdone, Paul. *The Little Red Hen.* Scholastic, 1973.

Galdone, Paul. *The Three Bears.* Scholastic, 1973.

Galdone, Paul. *The Three Little Pigs.* Clarion, 1970.

Hands, Hargrave. First Look Nature Books. Grosset and Dunlap, 1985.

Hoban, Tana. *Big Ones, Little Ones.* Greenwillow, 1976.

Hoban, Tana. *Is It Red? Is It Yellow? Is It Blue?* Greenwillow, 1978.

Hoberman, Mary Ann. *A House Is a House for Me.* Big Book. Scholastic, 1985.

Hogrogrian, Nonny. *One Fine Day.* Macmillan, 1971.

Hughes, Shirley. *Noisy.* Lothrop, Lee and Shepard, 1985.

Hutchins, Pat. *The Doorbell Rang.* Greenwillow, 1986.

Hutchins, Pat. *Good-Night, Owl!* Macmillan, 1972.

Isadora, Rachel. *I See.* Greenwillow, 1985.

Langstaff, John. *Oh, A-Hunting We Will Go.* Atheneum, 1974.

Lilly, Kenneth. *Animal Swimmers.* Random House, 1984.

Lilly, Kenneth. Baby Animal Board Books. Simon and Schuster, 1982.

Lionni, Leo. *Swimmy.* Pantheon, 1963.

Mack, Stan. *10 Bears in My Bed.* Pantheon, 1974.

Martin Bill Jr. *Brown Bear, Brown Bear, What Do You See?* Illustrated by Eric Carle. Holt, Rinehart and Winston, 1983.

Ormerod, Jan. *Silly Goose.* Lothrop, Lee and Shepard, 1986.

Peek, Merle. *Mary Wore Her Red Dress and Henry Wore His Green Sneakers.* Clarion, 1985.

Provensen, Alice, and Martin Provensen. *A Peaceable Kingdom: The Shaker Abecedarius.* Viking, 1978.

Rockwell, Anne. *Cars.* Dutton, 1984.

Sendak, Maurice. *Chicken Soup with Rice.* Harper and Row, 1962.

Spier, Peter. *London Bridge Is Falling Down!* Doubleday, 1967.

Stanley, Diane Zuromskis. *Fiddle-I-Fee.* Little, Brown, 1979.

Wildsmith, Brian. *Brian Wildsmith's Mother Goose.* Watts, 1964.

Wright Story Box Program. *Mrs. Wishy-Washy.* Big Book. Wright Group Publishing, 1984.

Zuromskis, Diane. *Farmer in the Dell.* Little, Brown, 1978.

Teaching Higher Order Reading Skills with Literature: Primary Grades

Lee Galda

Attending to Details and Making Inferences

- Book: *You'll Soon Grow into Them, Titch* by Pat Hutchins (Greenwillow, 1983)
- These questions are designed to help early elementary readers notice details in illustrations and make inferences based on these visual details. The procedure is appropriate for use with picture books in which the illustrations provide information not stated in the text. In *You'll Soon Grow into Them, Titch,* the illustrations convey the passage of time.
- Hold the book so all students can see the illustrations. After the title page has been read,

> SAY: Look at this picture to see Titch and signs of the season (first page of text/illustration). What do you see in this picture? (Small boy whose pants won't button, bird on tree with buds, bare dirt, plants beginning to come up in bowl, mom with chubby tummy knitting small pants.)
>
> DO: Read the text up to the fourth illustration.
>
> SAY: Tell me what you see in this picture. (Boy with sweater too small, leaves on trees are coming out, bird is sitting on nest, plants coming up outside, mother obviously pregnant and knitting a baby sweater.)
>
> SAY: What things have changed since the first picture? What can you tell is happening?
>
> DO: Read the text to the sixth picture. Ask the same questions. Read to the tenth picture and repeat the process.
>
> SAY: What evidence do you see that shows time is passing?

Illustration from *You'll Soon Grow into Them, Titch* by Pat Hutchins. Copyright © 1983 by Pat Hutchins. Greenwillow Books, a division of William Morrow & Company, Inc. Reprinted by permission.

Inferring Character Traits

- Book: *Miss Maggie* by Cynthia Rylant, illustrated by Thomas Di Grazia (Dutton, 1983)
- This activity is designed to help students recognize character traits and relationships among characters. They will recognize changes in those traits and relationships as the book progresses. The activity is appropriate to use with any book in which the main character is well developed.
- After you have read the story (perhaps earlier in the day) reread the first five pages.

    SAY: Who are the main characters? (Who is the story about?)
    DO: Write their names on the board or a chart, leaving plenty of space between them.
    SAY: What is each person like?
    DO: Write descriptors under names and draw a box around each name with its descriptors.
    SAY: How did they feel about one another?
    DO: Write responses on arrows running from box to box. The result will resemble this:

```
┌──────────┐                                    ┌──────────────┐
│ NAT      │      scared, curious about snake   │ MISS MAGGIE  │
│ young    │ ─────────────────────────────────▶ │ old          │
│ curious  │           nice to him              │ strange      │
│          │ ◀───────────────────────────────── │ scary        │
└──────────┘                                    └──────────────┘
```

    DO: Continue rereading the story. Follow the same procedure, focusing on the end of the story. Then compare the two charts. Discuss the changes in the characters and their relationships and the reasons for these changes.

*From **Miss Maggie** by Cynthia Rylant, illustrated by Thomas DiGrazia. Illustrations copyright © 1983 by Thomas DiGrazia. Reproduced by permission of the publisher, E.P. Dutton, a division of New American Library.*

Based on an idea by A. Butler and J. Turbill, *Towards a Reading—Writing Classroom*, PETA (Heinemann), 1984.

Recognizing Story Sequence and Cause and Effect

- Book: *Where the Wild Things Are* by Maurice Sendak (Harper & Row, 1963)

- This story-mapping activity is designed to help early readers develop a basic understanding of plot. The example used here is a simple one for beginning readers. Much folklore and other stories with simple plots would serve the same purpose.

- Read the story aloud.
   SAY: What happened in the story?
   DO: Write events on board or chart, adding any that the children leave out.
   SAY: What happened first/second/etc.?
   DO: Arrange the events clockwise, beginning slightly to the right of the top. The result will look something like this:

   DO: Draw arrows clockwise from one box to another, reading each item. If you wish to discuss cause and effect, you can label the boxes with "c" or "e" as appropriate.

- The same results also may be obtained by drawing a large circle, dividing the circle into one segment for each event, and allowing the children to draw or write the events in each segment. The result will look something like this:

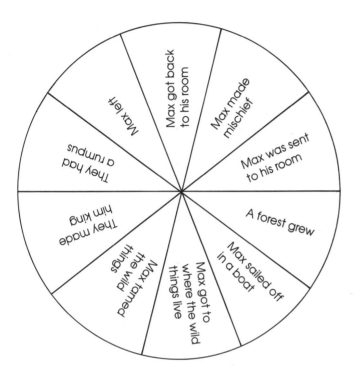

This version is especially appropriate for stories that begin and end in the same place.

Adapted from ideas by D. Ray Reutzel ("Story Maps Improve Comprehension." *The Reading Teacher,* 1985, *38,* 400-404) and Mary Jett-Simpson, ("Writing Stories Using Model Structures: The Circle Story." *Language Arts,* 1981, *58,* 293-300).

Section 3
Children's Literature in the Intermediate Grades

Children in the intermediate grades (4 to 6) need to try their wings by reading a wide variety of materials. Rudine Sims Bishop shows how many books can be used to develop multicultural understandings. She gives specific teaching ideas for using informational books, biography, folklore, realism, poetry, and fantasy. Dorothy Strickland describes two strategies–dialogue letters and story structure frameworks–that can be used with many kinds of books. Sam Sebesta expands the vision of the reading teacher to include art, drama, and literature. He presents ideas for enriching the visual arts, for involving children in drama, and for reflecting upon their experiences through journal writing.

Chapter 6
Extending Multicultural Understanding through Children's Books

Rudine Sims Bishop

Contrary to popular belief, the people of the United States have not been homogenized in a melting pot. While we all share some common experiences, many of the diverse groups that make up the country maintain distinctive cultural traditions and experiences. It is a multicultural society.

Literature can develop and extend at least three major understandings important to living in a multicultural society. First, literature can show how we are connected to one another through our emotions, our needs, our desires–experiences common to all. Understanding our common humanity is a powerful weapon against the forces that would divide and alienate us from one another.

Second and coincidentally, books can help us to understand, appreciate, and celebrate the differences among us–those things that make each cultural group special and enrich the larger society by adding distinctive flavors to the "salad bowl" of our common nationality.

Third, literature can be used to develop an understanding of the effects of social issues and forces on the lives of ordinary individuals. In the United States, as in many societies, there are social issues that must be faced if our major problems are to be solved. Racism and poverty are two of the worst problems, and they disproportionately victimize people who are members of nonwhite minority groups. Inevitably, some of the books that center on characters from those groups deal with such social issues. Through the experience of reading, and thereby sharing briefly in the lives of the characters, young people come to understand the potentially devastating effects of negative forces on our everyday lives.

Children's literature is also one of the ways we transmit our values to young people. It lets them know what adults consider appropriate ways of behaving, believing, and valuing, as well as who and what we consider important. Children who find their own life experiences mirrored in books receive an affirmation of themselves and their culture. Children who find that people like themselves are excluded or denigrated receive another message altogether. They learn that they are not valued members of society and that reading can be a negative or hurtful experience.

No more than twenty-five years ago, with few exceptions, children's literature treated U.S. minority cultures in one of two ways. They were either excluded and ignored or cast as comic relief, objects of ridicule, or blatant stereotypes. As a result of the Civil Rights Movement, and partly as a result of the Elementary and Secondary Education Act, that situation changed during the middle and late 1970s. Relatively large numbers of books about blacks appeared, and more positive and authentic images were presented. Although books about blacks represented the largest number, books about other minority groups–such as Latinos, Native Americans, and Asian Americans–also became more plentiful during the 1970s.

Unfortunately, in the 1980s, fewer books have been published about U.S. minority cultures. By the mid 1980s, only about 1 percent of children's books being published yearly were about blacks, and the picture was even more dismal for other groups. For example, from 1972 to 1982, a total of only 56 children's books about Puerto Ricans were published. The good news is that a number of good quality books are still available about minority cultures (particularly blacks) in the United States. Even though many books of the 70s are out of print, they are often available in libraries.

The remainder of this chapter will discuss some of the ways such books can be used in classrooms, particularly in the intermediate and upper grades.

Nonfiction: Starting with Information

Understanding requires knowledge. A logical place to begin developing multicultural understanding is with nonfiction. One excellent book that represents black history through primary source materials is Lester's Newbery Honor Book *To Be a Slave,* which excerpts narratives elicited from former slaves. It covers the period from 1619 through Reconstruction. Milton Meltzer, a historian and biographer, has produced some of the best nonfiction about minorities. His *The Black Americans: A History in Their Own Words* (Meltzer) is a compilation of primary source materials–diaries, journals, speeches, newspaper accounts, and letters–that tell the history of black Americans from 1619 to 1983. Meltzer has also has written books about other groups: *The Hispanic Americans, The Chinese Americans, The Jewish Americans: A History in Their Own Words,* and *Taking Root: Jewish Immigrants in America.* These books and others like them can provide much needed factual information for pupils studying American history. Along with historical fiction, they can provide richer, more detailed information about some of the groups that make up the country.

Activities Using History

Aside from the usual written or oral reports, books about various cultural groups lend themselves to other kinds of activities.

- The dramatic story of the Chinese workers who built the railroads in the West (*The Chinese Americans,* pp. 13-23) would make a fine mural.
- Uppergrade students can present information about several groups in chart form, indicating such information as where the groups emigrated from, what conditions caused them to leave home, where they settled initially in the United States, what kind of work they did, etc.
- Books that present personal narratives might serve as models for older students, who might try to collect some oral histories from people in their community who have memories of the immigrant experience.

These books are best read and discussed as a part of an integrated curriculum unit on U.S. history, rather than being confined to certain holidays or commemorations or restricted to classrooms in which the groups being studied are represented in the student body.

Biographies also help to develop understandings about the lives of members of different cultural groups and their contributions to the larger society. The following sources may be consulted for help in finding biographies about people from nonwhite cultures: *The Black Experience in Children's Books* (Rollock, 1984), *Literature by and about the American Indian* (Stensland, 1979), *Your Reading: A Booklist for Junior High and Middle School Students* (Christensen, 1983), *Interracial Books for Children Bulletin* (vol. 14, nos. 1 and 2 for Puerto Ricans, Nieto, 1983). In addition, *Portraits: Biography and Autobiography in the Secondary School* (Fleming & McGinnis, 1985) presents several ways to approach biography in the classroom and includes discussion questions and classroom activities.

Folklore

Every cultural group has developed a folklore. Folktales can give insight into the collective traditional dreams, values, humor, and other characteristics of a group. Furthermore, folktales are good stories, suitable for all ages. Any classroom in which there is a concern about multicultural understanding should have available an abundance of folktales. Many collections can be found in local libraries. In addition, single tales in picture book format can be used with older students, particularly when the tale is unfamiliar.

Because folktales come from an oral tradition, they lend themselves to being read aloud. Sometimes, in an attempt to retain the flavor of the language of the original storytellers, the compiler of a collection of stories

Comparing Folktales

With older children, folktales from a number of cultural groups can be studied and compared.

- In black American folklore, the Bruh Rabbit character, brought from Africa and later replaced by the slave character John, is a trickster. (See "He Lion, Bruh Bear, and Bruh Rabbit" from *The People Could Fly.*) Students can look for tricksters in stories from other cultures and compare their exploits.

- *Juan Bobo and the Pig* (Chardiet), a Puerto Rican tale, is a kind of "noodlehead" story that can be compared to other such stories from various cultures.

- Black folklore also contains some "why" stories, for example, "Why Dogs Hate Cats" from Julius Lester's *The Knee-High Man and Other Tales*. These stories can be compared to why stories from other groups and can serve as models for students who might want to create their own explanations for phenomena they have observed.

Enjoying stories from different cultural groups and discussing their similarities and differences can be effective in fostering multicultural understandings.

*Illustration from **The People Could Fly: Black American Folktales** by Virginia Hamilton. Text copyright © 1985 by Virginia Hamilton, illustrations copyright © 1985 by Leo and Diane Dillon. Alfred A. Knopf, Inc. Reprinted by permission.*

uses a nonstandard dialect to tell the story. For example, in the introduction to *The People Could Fly,* Virginia Hamilton states: "I use a reasonably colloquial language or dialect, depending on the folktale. Moderate colloquialisms are understandable and readable. They reflect the expressiveness of the original slave teller, and later the free black storyteller" (p. xii). Sometimes teachers are concerned that they cannot adequately reproduce the dialect as written or that their attempts to read a story in a low prestige dialect will be seen as insulting or even racist. In the case of *The People Could Fly,* a bit of practice with a tape recorder and a conscious effort not to compound the colloquialisms presented in

Role Playing and Readers Theatre

An unusual biography that lends itself to a number of classroom activities is Eloise Greenfield's *Childtimes: A Three-Generation Memoir.* It tells of the "growing up times" of three women–grandmother, mother, daughter. Each woman tells her own story. The book lends itself well to role playing.

- Students could present episodes from the lives of each of the three women. Since the book retains the feel of real oral language, parts of it could be presented as Readers Theatre.
- It could also be the inspiration and model for similar books published by members of the class who interview their own parents or grandparents about special growing up memories and then add their own stories.

Teaching Idea

*Illustration from **Childtimes: A Three-Generation Memoir** by Eloise Greenfield and Lessie Jones Little, drawings by Jerry Pinkney. Copyright © 1979 by Eloise Greenfield and Lessie Jones Little. Copyright © 1971 by Pattie Ridley Jones. Reprinted by permission of Harper & Row, Publishers.*

the stories with an affected Southern accent might demonstrate that the stories are readable as written. Also, remember that the tales come from an oral tradition in which tellers add their own touches to the stories. The tales can be changed in the telling or in the reading. In any case, *The People Could Fly* should not be missed.

Realistic Fiction

The largest group of books about minorities falls into the category of realistic fiction. This is the literature that describes life as it is today (or in the case of historical fiction, as it was yesterday) and provides readers with insights about what it takes to be a respectable

Teaching Idea

Discussing Realistic Fiction

In the classroom, it is important to share realistic fiction with students.
- Read a book aloud one chapter at a time, then discuss it with the students.
- If multiple copies of a book are available, students can read individually and form groups in which they discuss their responses to the books and respond to teacher developed questions. Such questions should be open-ended and not require one right answer. These might include the following:
  - Why do you suppose the main character responded the way he or she did to the conflict in the book?
  - What might have been an alternative response?
  - How might the main character's experience been different if he or she had not been a member of a minority group?
  - How does this book remind you of (give name)?
  - What does the title mean to you?
  - Responses to these questions will reveal how the reader uses previous information to predict and infer from text.
  - In addition, realistic fiction can help students become more aware of the literary elements in a book.
- For example, discuss the way Virginia Hamilton uses flashbacks in *Sweet Whispers, Brother Rush* to help students discover the ways plots can be structured.
- The same book lends itself to a discussion of the way characterization can be developed. M'Vy, the mother of Teresa and Dabney, does not actually appear in the book until page 89, yet the reader has built a clear picture of her up to that point through the flashbacks and through Teresa's thoughts.
- Discuss the author's expression of theme by asking students to find passages in which characters' statements might be considered a theme for the book. For instance, on page 209, Tree is told, "I found out you can't run away from what you've lost, or what you love, either...." Ask students to find other passages that express different themes.

individual in their society. In the case of realistic fiction about a minority group, it is often true that the best attempts to mirror and illuminate the experiences of growing up a member of that group will come from authors who are members of the group.

In the past two decades, a number of black writers have produced realistic fiction about blacks. Two such writers, Virginia Hamilton and Mildred Taylor, have been awarded the Newbery Medal. Others (for example, Lucille Clifton, Eloise Greenfield, Walter Dean Myers, Rosa Guy, Brenda Wilkinson, Sharon Bell Mathis, and Mildred Pitts Walter) have produced a body of good quality literature for intermediate and young adult readers.

There are fewer writers from other minority groups being published currently. Lawrence Yep, a Chinese-American, has produced a number of novels, some of which focus on growing up Chinese-American in the contemporary U.S., for example, *Sea Glass, Child of the Owl,* and *Dragonwings.* In *The Year of the Boar and Jackie Robinson,* Betty Bao Lord tells the story of a young Chinese immigrant growing up in Brooklyn. Virginia Driving Hawk Sneve writes about modern Native Americans (*When Thunders Spoke, Jimmy Yellow Hawk, High Elk's Treasure*). Jamake Highwater's fiction and nonfiction books about Native Americans, such as the Ghost Horse Cycle, are suitable for use with older readers. Yoshiko Uchida writes of the experiences of Japanese-Americans in the depression years in *A Jar of Dreams, The Best Bad Thing,* and *The Happiest Ending.* She describes the relocation camps of World War II in *Journey to Topaz* and their aftermath in *Journey Home.* Nicholasa Mohr wrote *Nilda* and *In Nueva York,* novels about growing up Puerto Rican in New York City.

Poetry and Fantasy

There is little poetry or fantasy available by and about minority groups, particularly for older students. However, that that is available should be located and incorporated into the classroom literature program. One fine collection of poetry is *Don't You Turn Back: Poems by Langston Hughes,* edited by Lee Bennett Hopkins. Because Hughes was greatly influenced by the rhythms of jazz and blues, his poetry lends itself easily to activities combining music and poetry. Dorothy Strickland collected both prose and poetry in *Listen Children: An Anthology of Black Literature. The Trees Stand Shining: Poetry of the North American Indians,* selected by Hettie Jones, is a collection of songs that have been sung for many years.

Walter Dean Myers wrote a fantasy, *The Legend of Tarik,* about a black North African knight. Virginia Hamilton produced a historical fantasy entitled *The Magical Adventures of Pretty Pearl.* These books should be included among fantasies being shared in the classroom.

Conclusion

Reading is an active experience. Each time we read a good piece of literature, we are changed by the experience; we see the world in a new way. It is this capacity to change us, to change our perspective on the world, that makes literature a vehicle for understanding cultures and experiences different from our own. Teachers who incorporate literature from various cultures into the classroom can contribute to making tomorrow's world more humane and considerate.

References

Christensen, Jane (Ed.). *Your reading: A booklist for junior high and middle school students.* Urbana, IL: National Council of Teachers of English, 1983.

Fleming, Margaret, and McGinnis, Jo (Eds.). *Portraits: Biography and autobiography in the secondary school.* Urbana, IL: National Council of Teachers of English, 1985.

Nieto, Sonia (Guest Editor). Puerto Ricans in children's literature and history texts: A ten year update. *Interracial Books for Children Bulletin,* 1983, *14,* Nos. 1 and 2.

Rollock, Barbara. *The black experience in children's books.* New York: New York Public Library, 1984.

Stensland, Anna Lee. *Literature by and about the American Indian,* new edition. Urbana, IL: National Council of Teachers of English, 1979.

Children's Books

Chardiet, Bernice. *Juan Bobo and the Pig: A Puerto Rican Folktale Retold.* Walker, 1973.

Greenfield, Eloise, and Lessie Jones Little. *Childtimes: A Three-Generation Memoir.* Crowell, 1979.

Hamilton, Virginia. *The Magical Adventures of Pretty Pearl.* Harper and Row, 1983.

Hamilton, Virginia. *The People Could Fly: American Black Folktales.* Knopf, 1985.

Hamilton, Virginia. *Sweet Whispers, Brother Rush.* Philomel, 1982.

Highwater, Jamake. *Legend Days.* Part One of the Ghost Horse Cycle. Harper and Row, 1984.

Highwater, Jamake. *Ceremony of Innocence.* Part Two of the Ghost Horse Cycle. Harper and Row, 1985.

Hopkins, Lee Bennett (Ed.) *Don't You Turn Back: Poems by Langston Hughes.* Knopf, 1969.

Jones, Hettie (Selector). *The Trees Stand Shining: Poetry of the North American Indians.* Dial, 1971.

Lester, Julius. *The Knee-High Man and Other Tales.* Dial, 1972.

Lester, Julius. *To Be a Slave.* Dell, 1968.

Lord, Betty Bao. *The Year of the Boar and Jackie Robinson.* Harper and Row, 1984.

Meltzer, Milton. *The Black Americans: A History in Their Own Words.* Crowell, 1984.

Meltzer, Milton. *The Chinese Americans.* Crowell, 1980.

Meltzer, Milton. *The Hispanic Americans.* Crowell, 1982.

Meltzer, Milton. *The Jewish Americans: A History in Their Own Words.* Crowell, 1982.

Meltzer, Milton. *Taking Root: Jewish Immigrants in America.* Farrar, Straus and Giroux, 1976.

Mohr, Nicholasa. *In Nueva York.* Dell, 1977.

Mohr, Nicholasa. *Nilda.* Harper and Row, 1983.

Myers, Walter Dean. *The Legend of Tarik.* Scholastic, 1982.

Sneve, Virginia Driving Hawk. *High Elk's Treasure.* Holiday, 1972.

Sneve, Virginia Driving Hawk. *Jimmy Yellow Hawk.* Holiday, 1972.

Sneve, Virginia Driving Hawk. *When Thunders Spoke.* Holiday, 1974.

Strickland, Dorothy S. *Listen Children: An Anthology of Black Literature.* Bantam, 1982.

Uchida, Yoshiko. *The Best Bad Thing.* McElderry, 1983.

Uchida, Yoshiko. *The Happiest Ending.* McElderry, 1985.

Uchida, Yoshiko. *A Jar of Dreams.* McElderry, 1981.

Uchida, Yoshiko. *Journey Home.* McElderry, 1979.

Uchida, Yoshiko. *Journey to Topaz.* Scribner's, 1971.

Yep, Lawrence. *Child of the Owl.* Harper and Row, 1977.

Yep, Lawrence. *Dragonwings.* Harper and Row, 1975.

Yep, Lawrence. *Sea Glass.* Harper and Row, 1979.

Additional Children's Books about Minority Groups

Belpre, Pura. *Santiago.* Warne, 1969.

Binzen, Bill. *Miguel's Mountain.* Coward-McCann, 1968.

Boyd, Candy. *Breadsticks and Blessing Places.* Macmillan, 1985.

Buck, Pearl S. *The Big Wave.* Curtis, 1947.

Bunting, Eve. *The Happy Funeral.* Harper and Row, 1982.

Clifton, Lucille. *Everett Anderson's Good-Bye.* Holt, 1983.

Friedman, Ian R. *How My Parents Learned to Eat.* Houghton Mifflin, 1984.

Hamilton, Virginia. *A Little Love.* Philomel, 1984.

Hamilton, Virginia. *Willie Bea and the Time the Martians Landed.* Greenwillow, 1983.

Houston, Jeanne Wakatsuki, and James D. Houston. *Farewell to Manzanar.* Houghton Mifflin, 1973.

Hunter, Kristin. *Lou in the Limelight.* Scribner's 1981.

Lester, Julius. *This Strange New Feeling.* Dial, 1982.

Mohr, Nicholasa. *Going Home.* Dial, 1986.

Myers, Walter Dean. *Hoops.* Delacorte, 1981.

Myers, Walter Dean. *Motown and Didi.* Viking, 1984.

Myers, Walter Dean. *Won't Know Till I Get There.* Viking, 1982.

Taylor, Mildred. *Let the Circle Be Unbroken.* Dial, 1981.

Thomas, Joyce Carol. *Bright Shadow.* Avon, 1983.

Thomas, Joyce Carol. *Marked by Fire.* Avon, 1982.

Walter, Mildred Pitts. *Because We Are.* Lothrop, 1983.

Walter, Mildred Pitts. *Trouble's Child.* Lothrop, 1985.

Yashima, Taro. *Umbrella.* Viking, 1958.

Yashima, Taro, and Mitsui Yashima. *Momo's Kitten.* Viking, 1955.

Chapter 7

Literature: Key Element in the Language and Reading Program

Dorothy S. Strickland

"But Dr. Strickland, I'm so busy teaching reading that there is no time left for literature. And now they want me to teach more writing too." That statement, made by a competent, caring, but somewhat frustrated classroom teacher, is not unusual. Teachers care about providing their students with quality experiences with literature. Teachers know the importance of literature, but are unsure of its role in the language arts program. They want to know if trade books should serve primarily as support to basal readers. They ask whether literature plays a part in the writing program and how it can assist in the development of oral language. Most of all, teachers are interested in how literature can be used to help integrate the language arts.

These questions reflect the constraints of language arts curricula, which frequently isolate the teaching of reading, writing, listening, and speaking. Because of that isolation, teachers often perceive any attempt to initiate a more comprehensive literature program as adding yet another layer or another course of study to an already overloaded schedule.

The strategies in this chapter–Dialogue Letters and a Story Structure Framework for Reading and Writing–exemplify the unifying role literature and literature related experiences can play in the language arts program. These strategies are long term, ongoing practices for the language arts curriculum, rather than specific activities for use with particular books. They demonstrate the influence literary experiences can have on the development of skill in listening, speaking, reading, and writing. The chapter concludes with guidelines for developing literature based language arts strategies.

Dialogue Letters

Donna Carrara, a fourth grade teacher in New Jersey, reaches for a letter in a folder on her desk. She reads:

Dear Mrs. Carrara
I like my book because it is weird and funny also it's got a little mystery. The lead wasn't really pulling me in but I still wanted to read it. What I think is going to happen is Milo finds the Mathemagican It's about a boy whom isn't that smart and one day he gets a package which doesn't say where it's from and then he gets into another time zone. The arthur is Norton Juster and the title is the Phanton Tollbooth. I love the book it's great.

from,

Jimmy

She takes a clean sheet of paper and responds:

Dear Jimmy,

I was very surprised that the lead didn't pull you in. What did make you want to read the book?

The author seems to be saying that Milo must assume responsibility for learning. It's interesting how authors have messages in their books.

I got the feeling that Milo entered another world as well as a time zone. Authors seem to be fascinated with this topic. A wrinkle in Time—The Chronicles of Narnia are just a few of these types of books.

I'll be anxious to hear if Milo finds the Mathe-magician.

I sense the author uses a little of the fairy tale element in this book. What do you think?

Mrs Carrera

This sample of correspondence between teacher and student comes from a classroom where activities centered around literature are a natural part of each day's activities. These children read numerous books throughout the year and respond to their reading in various ways; e.g., write letters to the teacher when beginning or completing a book. Each letter receives a personal response.

How Do Dialogue Letters Teach Reading?

The letters establish a dialogue between teacher and student about something of interest to both. Students write about something they care about to someone who supports what they are doing and saying and who manages to challenge them. Students like writing to share their ideas with a real person and being able to count on a response. They are told to concentrate on the content of their letters. Although they are urged to re-read and revise in order to be certain their message is clear, students know their teacher's response will not focus on the mechanics of their communication. The response always focuses on what pupils are attempting to say rather than how they say it.

As the months pass, Donna notes growth in the degree of comprehension and reflection the letters convey. Students begin to apply what they have learned in other language arts activities. For example, they often share personal motives for selecting a particular book. In his letter, Jimmy tells why he stuck with his book even though "the lead wasn't pulling me in." Donna feels this statement stems from several discussions during writing workshop where she and the students talked about what makes a good lead. She is pleased that students not only think about good leads when they write, but are also con-

scious of them in someone else's writing. Moreover, she is pleased that they are applying what they have learned from one setting to another.

In their letters, students offer a wide variety of reasons for selecting a book–topic, genre, favorite author, a friend's recommendation, a recommendation from the teacher or librarian, a television show, or an enticing book jacket.

The many reasons students give for selecting a book remind us of how important it is to expose children to literature in a variety of ways. Often, the first exposure to a particular author or genre is through the daily read aloud time. Writing workshops and sharing sessions, where students share what they are reading and writing, offer other opportunities for them to talk about literature.

Often, letters students write as they start a book include predictions about events in the story: "What I think is going to happen is Milo finds the Mathemagician." Often students refer to these predictions again in the final letter and give reasons they were or were not confirmed. Whether children are reading stories or learning from a science or social studies text, making and confirming predictions are important parts of the reading program in this classroom. Students are applying what they have learned in a functional way.

Donna uses her responses as a tool for individualizing instruction. Through the dialogue letters, she focuses on each individual's special interests and manner of expression. Her letters support the students' ideas and opinions; her questions and comments make them think in new ways and leave them with additional options to consider. She refers to other literature in her letters, comparing and contrasting various titles and authors. She also models strategies students might find valuable in their own reading, writing, and thinking.

Dialogue letters about books students read independently may be easily adapted to any classroom. The letters stimulate students to read.

Story Structure Framework for Reading and Writing

Researchers studying the development of story in children and those studying the structure or grammar of stories have linked their findings to children's development of reading and writing. The role of prior knowledge and experience in reading and writing suggests that learners who have had many experiences with stories and have developed a strong schema for stories make use of that framework as they read and write (Strickland & Feeley, 1986, p. 166).

Joan Feeley and I developed The Story Structure Framework for Reading and Writing in an attempt to combine in one comprehensive plan some of the best strategies for developing children's sense of story while offering them opportunities to apply that knowledge to their reading and writing. The plan involves three phases: exposure to and discussion of stories within a particular genre; retelling and reconstructing stories within the genre; and writing activities focused on the genre.

Story Structure: Exploring the Genre

The first time Sam Greene, a teacher in Connecticut, used the Story Structure Framework, he introduced Greek Myths to his fifth graders. The study of ancient Greece is a major part of the social studies program at this level. Marsha Sarno, a New York City teacher, got her sixth graders deeply immersed in mystery stories during her first attempt at using the model. Her decision to begin with mys-

teries came as a result of interest demonstrated by several members of the class. Donna Carrara shared Indian legends with her fourth graders in conjunction with a social studies unit on the Lenne Lanape Indians of New Jersey. In each case, teachers selected materials within the genre to read aloud over a period of time.

Sam Greene reads to his class *Hercules* by Bernard Evslin and *The Olympians: Great Gods and Godesses of Ancient Greece* by L.E. Fisher. During this phase, the teacher and the librarian present "book talks" about books in the same genre and encourage students to select books for independent reading. Both reading aloud by the teacher and independent reading by the children are accompanied by group discussions and personalized conferences focused on the elements of story. Questions related to setting and characterization, initiating events, goals, major actions, conclusions, and the reader's personal reactions and responses are used to further story comprehension and appreciation. For example, during the reading of *Hercules* (Evslin), these types of questions might be used:

"Now that _____ has reached his goal, what do you think will happen?" (predicting characters' behavior, predicting events)

"Now that the author has described the setting of this story, can you close your eyes and see it? Describe what you see. (visualizing word pictures, predicting images)

"Why do you suppose _____ reacted the way she did when she discovered what her friend did? (stating character motives)

Story Structure: Oral Responses

A second phase of the plan overlaps the first. It involves engaging students in various follow up activities to the reading. Many

*Illustration from **Hercules** by Bernard Evslin, illustrated by Jos. A. Smith. Illustrations copyright © 1984 by Jos. A. Smith. William Morrow and Company, Inc. Reprinted by permission.*

teachers choose to involve students in an extended discussion based on major events or actions in a story. Others select creative dramatics or story retellings as a postreading activity. Whatever activity is selected, it should involve students in reflecting on and recreating the story in some way or in projecting alternative outcomes to those in the text. If extended discussion is selected as a postreading activity, the following types of questions might be used:

"What do you suppose would have happened if...?" (predicting alternative outcomes based on a change in an initiating event)

"What did _____ try that did not work? What else did _____ try?" (recounting major problem solving events)

"In your opinion, did _____ react properly to _____?" (applying personal judgment to a character's motives and behavior)

"What else might _____ have done?" (suggesting alternate actions)

Some teachers use creative dramatics to

*Illustration from **The Olympians** by Leonard Everett Fisher. Copyright © 1984 by Leonard Everett Fisher. Holiday House. Reprinted by permission.*

follow story reading. Students pantomime scenes from the story, use Readers Theatre scripts, role play interesting characters, or act out specific scenes or entire stories. Discussing the characters, settings, and events prior to the dramatization helps prepare students for their roles.

If story retelling is selected, students may retell the story orally or in writing. When students retell the story in writing, they may select partners and compare their retellings to locate gaps and misstatements. They can return to the text to solve disagreements or to confirm what they both believe to be true. Whether students are dramatizing or retelling a story, they rely on aspects of story structure for recall and reconstruction.

Story Structure: Comprehending to Composing

The final phase of the plan involves a series of writing activities, moving from whole group shared writing to independent writing. By this time, students will have had a great deal of exposure to the genre under study. They will have listened to stories, read stories, discussed stories, dramatized stories, and re-told stories. Most students will have developed an implicit knowledge of the features associated with the type of stories they have been reading. Making this knowledge explicit is a good way to launch students into the writing phase. In order to do this, the teacher elicits from the students what they have learned about a biography, a tall tale, or a legend. They discuss what makes this type of story special or different from others. The accompanying chart about mystery stories was developed by Marsha Sarno's sixth graders.

Using the chart and their knowledge of story structure to guide them, the story writing proceeds as follows:

Shared retelling. Teacher and students may select a favorite story to retell in written form with the teacher as scribe. They compare elements with those on the chart.

Shared writing. Teacher and students create an original story. Again, teacher acts as scribe and models revision and editing.

Independent writing. Individuals are encouraged to include the genre in their story writing efforts and to share their stories with the group.

Following are examples of legends created by two of Donna Carrara's fourth graders:

What makes a Mystery Story

1. It has clues.
2. Something bad happens.
3. There is a character or group of characters who act like detectives.
4. Someone has to solve the crime.
5. Sometimes there is a surprise ending.
6. There are good guys and bad guys.
7. There is suspense.
8. It keeps you (the reader) guessing.
9. It is like an adventure story.

December 9, 1985

Beth

How The Tiger Got It's Stripes

One day a large tiger was walking through the forest. In his path there was a tree with hundreds of black vines hanging from it. The tiger walked through the vines. When he came out there were hundreds of black stripes on him. That's how the tiger got his stripes.

12/5/85

Julie

How the flowers got there colors.

once ther was a Lenapea that was colting berries. Well it just so happend that the Lenapea was very clumsy and he dropped all the berries and they smushed. Thear were seeds of flowers under them. When the flowers grew the berries stuck on top and stuck to it and thats how the flowers got thear color.

As the year progresses, students strengthen their knowledge of story structures and add to their repertoire the types of stories they feel confident reading and writing. Teachers using the plan recommend it as a useful vehicle for systematically introducing literature into the language arts program and as a basis for developing listening, speaking, reading, and writing skills.

Guidelines for Developing Literature Based Language Arts Strategies

Certain basic assumptions underlie the strategies offered in this chapter. As mentioned earlier, these strategies are not intended to be one time activities, perfect for a particular book and never used again. Instead, they are meant to be put in place as predictable yet flexible elements of the curriculum. Because they invite a variety of applications, these predictable frameworks offer students the potential for freedom of expression, creativity, and independence. The strategies are based upon certain assumptions about what is required in order that literature may work to bring together the language arts as a unified whole.

- Students have access to many books in their classroom library, school library, and public library. A plentiful and accessible literature resource is essential to a literature based language arts program.

- Time is set aside daily for independent reading in school. In order for students to view the self-selection and voluntary reading of books as an important part of their lives, these activities must not be assigned as homework or relegated to something to be done when work has been completed.

- Reading aloud to children from various types of literature is a regular part of the language arts program.

- Book talks and sharing sessions involving the discussion of books by teachers, librarians, and students are regular parts of reading and writing activities.

- There is a conscious effort to relate reading and writing instruction. Lessons during writing workshops feature examples from literature: how authors develop a plot, use interesting language, and create good leads and closings. Discussions during reading help students learn to read like writers.

- At times, there are several activities focusing on a single work of literature, a particular genre, or the work of a certain author or illustrator. Children need in-depth explorations into literature to extend their sense of story and to develop appreciation and understanding of literary works.

● Finally, students respond to literature in various ways. Responses may be written or oral, formal or informal. Students have opportunities to respond and share while they are reading as well as after they finish a book.

Teachers who initiate a planned literature program using these guidelines will reap unexpected benefits for both their students and themselves. By offering students strategies that embrace these principles and by surrounding them with good books, teachers will instill positive attitudes and habits related to literature. They will generate new and interesting applications to help keep the language arts program alive.

Reference

Strickland, Dorothy, and Feeley, Joan. Using children's concept of story to improve reading and writing. In T.L. Harris and E.J. Cooper (Eds.), *Reading, thinking, and concept development*. New York: College Board, 1985.

Children's Books

Evslin, Bernard. *Hercules.* Illustrated by Jos. A. Smith. William Morrow, 1984.

Fisher, L.E. *The Olympians: Great Gods and Goddesses of Ancient Greece.* Holiday House, 1984.

Juster, Norton. *The Phantom Tollbooth.* Random House, 1961.

Chapter 8
Enriching the Arts and Humanities through Children's Books

Sam Leaton Sebesta

John Dewey defined art as "an object which affords continuously renewed delight" (Dewey, 1929, p. 7). The definition can be expanded to include all the arts and humanities: objects and processes, experienced through language and other media, delighting us and enabling us to realize our humanity.

Dewey warned against false art under the guise of utility: "Innumerable commodities which are manufactured by the 'useful arts' are only apparently and superficially useful; their employment results not in satisfaction of intelligent desire, but in confusion and extravagance, bought at the price of a narrowed and embittered experience" (Dewey, 1929, p. 5).

Thus our mission is laid out for us. In busy classrooms, teaching children whose world is bombarded with those "innumerable commodities" that Dewey deplored, we must in-

clude the arts and humanities. Take heart! It is not a mission impossible, nor an interruption of the curriculum for developing practical skills–reading, writing, problem solving. Instead, the arts and humanities may yet be viewed as the means to integrate and energize the curriculum. Materials to achieve this mission are not scarce. They begin at our fingertips, with an open book. And the techniques we need are within every teacher's experience and creativity.

Children's Books and the Visual Arts

A good place to begin is with the role of the artist. Write "Artists Teach Us to See" on a large bulletin board and display prints of artists as varied as Picasso, Lichtenstein, and N.C. Wyeth. Observe that artists are not cameras

Looking at Art

- Place a heading—ARTISTS TEACH US TO SEE—at the top of a large bulletin board.
- Under the heading, display prints from a wide variety of artists.
- Discuss with students that art is not an exact representation of an object. Artists are interpreters who create meaning through their work.

Teaching Idea

Art as Interpretation

Guide students to an understanding that artists are interpreters of their world.
- Use M.B. Goffstein's *An Artist* to begin to develop the notion of the artist as interpreter.
- Follow up with a discussion of Chase's *Looking at Art,* which shows the many ways artists have interpreted one subject—the lion.

Teaching Idea

attempting to record a subject as everyone sees it. Instead, artists are interpreters who create meaning through an artistic product.

M.B. Goffstein's *An Artist* helps develop the understanding that art is interpretation. Her simple, succinct watercolors and text tell us that an artist "tries to shape beauty with his hand....He tries to make order out of nature." The idea is amplified in a classic book, *Looking at Art* by Alice Elizabeth Chase. Beginning with a photograph of a lion, the author shows how artists in various cultures have interpreted "lion"—the powerful, stylized lion of Assyrian bas-relief, the flowing grandeur of Durer's lion etching, Henri Rousseau's mystical lion bending over "The Sleeping Gypsy," and a vulnerable lion cub in Darrel Austin's painting. The book does not end there, but goes on to display the far from realistic visions of the cubists and surrealists, balanced against the decep-

tive realism of modern Gothic.

Books such as these help children do more than gaze at art. The art viewer's experience should not be so different from schema activation in reading comprehension or the engagement-involvement level of response to literature. To bring about this active viewing, try using interview techniques when children view an art object.

The role of the artist and intensive involvement with artworks converge when intermediate grade children compare and contrast picture books that show different artists' treatment of the same story. Tony Ross's *The Three Pigs,* for instance, updates the familiar tale uproariously: "Pig and his two friends, Pig and Pig, lived on the 39th floor of a city building." You can read this version aloud to older children—it's campy and never babyish. Ask them to sketch an illustration that captures the spirit of

Interview Technique 1

"You are the artist. What made you choose this subject? Why did you present it this way? How did you paint/draw/construct/sculpt this? What do you want people to 'see' in it?"

Such questions can spur interest in well-illustrated biographies of artists' lives:

- The "Art for Children" series by Ernest Raboff, which includes brief volumes about Paul Klee, Marc Chagall, and Pierre-Auguste Renoir;
- *Calder* (Bourdon), a nothing hidden biography of America's most innovative sculptor/mobilist;
- *I Carve Stone*, a photo filled visit to sculptor Joan Fine's studio.

Interview Technique 2

"You are there. You've walked into this picture. You are in the place where this art object first appeared. What do you see and hear? What's going on beyond the picture? What happens next, after this scene?"

This device is used by countless fantasy writers, including E. Nesbit, Philippa Pearce, and P.L. Travers (see, for instance, Chapter 2 in *Mary Poppins*). It encourages interaction with what might otherwise be one glance artworks.

- Try it with John Goodall's wordless picture book *The Story of an English Village* or the busy Italian town in Brian Wildsmith's *Give a Dog a Bone*.
- A unique volume showing *Pieter Brueghel's The Fair* in full panorama followed by enlarged detail provides a special invitation for this walk-into-the-picture experience. "See what you can find," invites the author, Ruth Craft. "Like all painters Pieter Brueghel took his time. Take yours."

Interview Technique 3

"If you talked with the character(s) in this artwork, what would you tell about yourself? How might you let them know that *your* life and *their* lives have something in common?"

The many volumes of Shirley Glubok's "The Art of..." series (e.g., *Art of Colonial America, The Art of Egypt under the Pharaohs,* and *Doll's Houses: Life in Miniature*) are especially suited to this interview technique.

*Illustration from **An Artist** by M.B. Goffstein. Copyright © 1980 by M.B. Goffstein. Harper & Row, Publishers. Reprinted by permission.*

this telling of the story, and then show them the Tony Ross pictures.

The many picture book versions of *Hansel and Gretel* (Grimm) will convince art viewers once and for all that artists are interpreters of the world. Susan Jeffers's repeated design of leaves and branches, sheltering harmless creatures, suggests that there is pattern and plan in this adventure of unwanted children. It's a world that protects children, after all. But

Lisbeth Zwerger doesn't see it that way. As the children go deeper into the forest, Zwerger's color wash becomes dark and menacing. The witch, shapeless and nonhuman, is the center of all evil. Even when she's disposed of, there's that dark, fearful forest to be avoided. Paul O. Zelinsky's oil paintings reveal with realistic detail a bleak world where even the moonlight and sunlight are chilled, where even the children's homecoming may not be a return to a Golden Age. Contrast these versions with the more cheerful, more distanced *Hansel and Gretel* illustrations of Adrienne Adams and Paul Galdone.

Once the study of contrast in art style is underway, children will have little difficulty finding other examples, including contrasting art in various editions of *The Wind in the Willows* (Grahame), *Alice in Wonderland* (Carroll), the fables of Aesop, and *A Child's Garden of Verses* (Stevenson). The aim isn't really to decide that one style is best but, rather, to discover that the close examination of illustrations opens new avenues to interpretation and new insight into the role of the artist.

Producing art as well as looking at it helps children find "continuously renewed delight." In *23 Varieties of Ethnic Art and How to Make Each One* (Kinney and Kinney) they'll find variety, all right–how to originate a Maggie and Jiggs type of comic strip; how to make Dutch tile, batik, origami, leatherwork, ice carving, and Swiss embroidery. An accompanying volume entitled *How to Make Whirligigs and Whimmy Diddles and Other American Folkcraft Objects* (Pettit) adds historical interest about how art has brought pleasure to generations of practical, hardworking Americans. Model building is explained with admirable detail and precision in *Wood Works: Experiments with Common Wood and Tools* (Brown) and a book on how to use throw-away bits and pieces to construct a *Make-Believe Empire* (Berman). There is even a book of patterns and photos of finished items to replicate ancient Egypt–*Egypt: Activities and Projects in Color* (Farnay and Soleillant). The array of children's books to instruct the child artist is limitless.

Children's Books and Drama

There are classrooms in which drama is integral to reading instruction. Children discuss a story as preparation to perform, and afterwards they discuss to evaluate the performance. Hence discussion gains purpose and pertinence through the arts of drama. Schema setting to present new words or to become familiar with a new concept is enlivened by drama. Prediction about what will happen in a selection to be read is done through drama rather than just talk. Book reports based on voluntary reading are enhanced by drama: pantomiming a crucial scene, reading dialogue as if it were a radio script, interviewing a character.

How are these classrooms prepared? How is drama presented so that it is approached with excitement, the will to do one's best, and a payoff in attitude and achievement? How do successful intermediate grade teachers make drama meaningful–a celebration of the arts, rather than a time of showing off or embarrassment?

Teachers begin with small segments, emphasizing mime. One teacher asked whether anyone would mime the scene from *Johnny Tremain* (Forbes) in which the hero burns his hand. There was silence. Then the teacher asked for help to move a table so there could be space for the performance. Volunteers came at once. "Before you sit back down," said the teacher, "help me sweep the floor so we can have a clean stage." She handed an imaginary broom to each volunteer and, without a word, began to mime sweeping. In this way, children became involved in mime that held no threat. Later, emphasis was placed on accuracy: The class reread the pertinent incident in *Johnny Tremain* (Chapter 2) to find out exactly what happened as a basis for the mime. Before long, volunteers were plentiful, each determined to improve on accuracy of the playing.

Teachers select material carefully and match technique to the material. Stories and narrative poems containing much action are best for mime. If the story is read or told as it is mimed, the technique is known as Story Theatre. Traditional tales, including _Heaven's Reward: Fairy Tales from China_ (Sadler) and _The Brocaded Slipper and Other Vietnamese Tales_ (Vuong) as well as the more familiar tales of the Western hemisphere, are naturals for Story Theatre. So, too,

*Illustration by **Cheng Mung Yun** from Heaven's Reward. Illustration copyright © 1985 Cheng Mung Yun. Reproduced with the permission of Atheneum Publishers, Inc.*

Sebesta

are classic story poems including "Little Orphant Annie," "The Tale of Custard the Dragon," and "Casey at the Bat."

If a story contains long stretches of plot determining dialogue, chances are that mime and Story Theatre are inappropriate. Instead, use the technique called Readers Theatre. Students select roles and read the dialogue as the characters would speak it, interspersed with reading by narrators who describe the action. Scripts for Readers Theatre may be adapted on the spot, simply by marking with a pencil dialogue lines in the story, or a catalog of scripts can be obtained from Institute for Readers Theatre, Box 17193, San Diego, California 92117.

Readers Theatre takes practice if it is not to sound like Round Robin reading. Instead of starting practice by reading lines aloud, have students mime the characters they're to portray and make up speeches that the characters might say. In other words, they are building character *before* they approach actual dialogue.

Mime and dialogue reading (done, respectively, through Story Theatre and Readers Theatre) are basic techniques. They can be expanded into creative dramatics (Siks, 1983) and fully staged play productions (Judy & Judy, 1982).

Teachers who successfully use drama techniques within the curriculum aren't likely to go outside the curriculum to find drama scripts, nor are they likely to devote large blocks of school time to polish a production to impress an audience. Drama in such classrooms is a process for teaching imagery, characterization, close reading for interpretation, and enhancing literacy experience. One fourth grade teacher has had tremendous success with Story Theatre using every one of the selections in Alice Low's *The Macmillan Book of Greek Gods and Heroes.* Another has had equally exciting results using an episode a day for Readers Theatre based on the works of Beverly Cleary, Lois Lowry, and Betsy Byars.

Drama in the Classroom

- Begin with small segments, emphasizing mime.
  Start with something easy, involving only a few actions to convey what is going on. Later move on to emphasize accuracy—have students reread the segment of a story to be dramatized in order to include all of the important details.
- Select material carefully and match technique to the material.
  In Story Theatre, the story is read or told as it is mimed. Readers Theatre is more appropriate for a story that includes large amounts of important dialogue. Each student selects a character to portray, and a narrator describes the action not conveyed by dialogue. Allow students plenty of time to practice either technique.
- Teach respect for theater as an art form.
  Make available many books, both fiction and nonfiction, that are about theater so students will understand the history and traditions surrounding theater.

Teaching Idea

Teachers teach respect for theatre as an art form. Knowing that theatre can be a source of lifelong delight in the humanities, teachers can prepare the way. Interest in how theatre works is aroused through books about the theater: *Make Your Own World of the Theater* (Lowndes and Kailer), a wonderful book of cutouts of stage sets for an opera and a ballet; Walter C. Hodges's fully pictured *Shakespeare's Theatre,* and Robert Lewis's book on the technicalities of acting, *Advice to Players.* Mary Ure's delightful fiction about trying out for a professional London production of *Little Women* (Alcott) is called *Supermouse,* and in *Stage Door to Terror* (Quackenbush) Miss Mallard, the famous "ducktective," solves a mystery behind the footlights.

Music, Movement, and the Sounds of Language

Drama and dance go hand in hand. I have demonstrated this connection in many intermediate grade classrooms and in assemblies. I select an African story such as "The Wedding of the Hawk" (Courlander), *Oh, Kojo! How Could You!* (Aardema), or *Why the Sun and the Moon Live in the Sky* (Dayrell). Sometimes I use "Momotaro" (Uchida), the Japanese epic aglitter with stolen jewels and an island of ogres. And there are countless other candidates (see, for instance, those collected in *The Family of Stories* by Moss and Stott).

First, my volunteers mime the story as I tell or read it. This requires coaching. A hawk must take off and land with care; a cat must show how the river courses over her as she walks across the river bottom; the dog, pheasant, and monkey must maintain their characteristic movements as they accompany Momo-

taro through the forest. After the story is mimed in this Story Theatre way, we dispense with the oral telling. We bring on the rhythm makers: a Nigerian drum, an African double drum, a Baule drum, a harp, and a Basonge bell–all constructed from household materials according to directions found in *African Crafts You Can Make* (D'Amato and D'Amato). When the mime is repeated to rhythmic beat, it takes on a different aspect. It becomes dance, with more exaggerated, repetitious movements.

Such a project ought to be followed by exposure to books about dance and the universal importance music has played in every culture. Rachel Isadora celebrates a child's debut in a big ballet production of "A Midsummer Night's Dream" in *Opening Night. Karen Kain: Born to Dance* (Zola) is a moving account of the struggles and ambitions of a ballerina. Robina Beckles Willson's *The Voice of Music* is a very readable history of music, with clear diagrams of almost every instrument.

And this is just the beginning. Children deserve more variety in music. They can learn plots of operas from the Curtain Raiser Books, which reveal that opera is neither dull nor silly. Karla Kuskin's *The Philharmonic Gets Dressed* shows children the ordinary preparations of the extraordinary players who perform in the Philharmonic Orchestra: "Their work is to play. Beautifully." They can look *Behind the Scenes of a Broadway Musical* (Powers), an entertaining written-for-children journal about the production of Maurice Sendak's "Really Rosie." They can discover the Mozart-like ebullience that transcends the troubled life of *Scott Joplin and the Ragtime Years* (Evans). Each one of these books is an invitation to listen to music.

*Illustration from **The Philhar-monic Gets Dressed** by Karla Kuskin, illustrations by Marc Simont. Text copyright © 1982 by Karla Kuskin, illustrations copyright © by Marc Simont. Harper & Row, Publishers. Reprinted by permission.*

Classroom teachers can have great influence on children's taste in music. One teacher experimented with a "Composer of the Month" plan. He began with Chopin in October, playing records of Chopin nocturnes, polonaises, and waltzes every day for at least an hour–quietly, as the class worked. Because so few good biographies of composers are available for children, he told about Chopin's life. He waited patiently. For ten days no one commented on the music. On the eleventh day a child said, "Could we have a little Chopin today during spelling?" By the end of the month, parents were busy obtaining Chopin records, marveling at their children's ability to recognize selections. November became Beethoven month. Eventually, students began searching through the pages of *Famous Names in Music: Bach to Britten* (Lewis) to plan programs for the rest of the school year.

Music and movement form a bridge to poetry, for, after all, poetry probably began as song. For most children, it's easier to sing a lyric than to read it aloud. For them, *The Moon on the One Hand: Poetry in Song* (Crofut) is a treasure. It contains wonderfully singable tunes to accompany Laura Richards's "Eletelephony" and selections by Robert Louis Stevenson, Hillaire Belloc, Randall Jarrell, and James Stephens. *I Am Phoenix: Poems for Two Voices* (Fleischman) is one step away from singing; it contains parallel poems to be read simultaneously, so the sound of language dominates over literal meaning.

There is a time when one realizes that every language has music in the way it is spoken. The street cries are replaced now by the lilt in a spoken commercial; the bard by a teacher, librarian, or parent who reads well aloud. Once every so often you say to yourself, "Ah! That was a line spoken well!" Once they are really listened to and implanted in the living memory, the sounds of music may be the basis for the sounds of language. Poetry or expressive prose perfectly spoken by an individual or a voice choir is a matchless gift. The child who performs or receives it is fortunate. It is at the heart of the humanities.

The Humanities and Journal Writing

Intermediate grade children are avid collectors. Ask a classroom of fourth graders "What do you collect?" and you'll be deluged with answers. Go back the next day and you'll be deluged with collections! One classroom I visited was different. When I asked about collections, each student hauled out a journal. "These are journals of experience," they said, looking profound. "We collect experience." And sure enough, behind the purple and gold university cover were eighty well-filled pages, front and back, in diary form—not about everyday happenings but about special happenings, about trips inward and outward to the arts and humanities.

These students had visited the University of Washington with their journals and viewed a massive, controversial sculpture called *Broken Obelisk*. One child wrote that it represented the triumphs and tragedies of space shuttle flight. Another speculated that it was the thunderbolt tossed to earth by Jupiter and Mars. One made it the setting of a mountain scaling expedition undertaken by a group of adventurous ants.

The journals recorded impressions of music listened to in the classroom and elsewhere. They reviewed a live theatre performance of "Theseus and the Minotaur," which the class had attended. In the back of one journal was an index of artworks and humanities experiences encountered by one student during the school year, placed succinctly under the title "The Things I've Seen and Heard."

There were also impressions based on reading—not just any reading but reading that struck the writers as a special never-to-be-forgotten experience. One student expressed surprise that he had read a whole book of poetry: Joanna Cole's *A New Treasury of Children's Poetry*. The child pointed out that the first poems in the book are easy but, as the book goes on, the poems get harder and more interesting. He copied one poem, Russell Hoban's "Jigsaw Puzzle," into his journal and wrote that this was the poem he had read to his dad. He said that his dad went around quoting the last line, "the world's like that too."

Some of the journal writers were thinking about becoming professional writers in a few years. They had formed an interest group to read about writers. They had read about the efforts of Jo March to write her melodramas in *Little Women* (Alcott) and about Louisa May Alcott's efforts to write about Jo March, described in *Invincible Louisa* (Meigs). They had read autobiographies about becoming a successful writer, including Lois Duncan's *Chapters: My Growth As a Writer* and M.E. Kerr's *Me! Me! Me! Me! Me!: Not a Novel*. They had read a novel called *A Long Way from Verona* (Gardam), all about Jessica Vye's determination to write, and Beverly Cleary's correspondence between reader and writer, *Dear Mr. Henshaw*. Their journals recorded the experience, the comfort of aspiring writers who find there are others like them, sharing their dreams of producing something wonderful.

These journals show a community of readers at work, pursuing the arts and humanities to find "continuously renewed delight." These children and others like them are gaining the best that education has to offer.

References

Dewey, John. Experience, nature, and art. *Art and education*. New York: Barnes, 1929, 3-12.

Judy, Susan, and Judy, Stephen. *Putting on a play*. New York: Scribner, 1982.

Siks, Geraldine Brain. *Drama with children*, second edition. New York: Harper and Row, 1983.

Children's Books

Aardema, Verna. *Oh, Kojo! How Could You!* Illustrated by Marc Brown. Dial, 1984.

Aesop Fables. Illustrated by Heide Holder. Viking, 1981.

Alcott, Louisa M. *Little Women*. Roberts Brothers, 1868, 1869.

Berman, Paul. *Make-Believe Empire: A How-to Book*. Atheneum, 1982.

Bourdon, David. *Calder: Mobilist, Ringmaster, Innovator*. Macmillan, 1980.

Brown, William F. *Wood Works: Experiments with Common Wood and Tools*. Illustrated by M.G. Brown. Atheneum, 1984.

Carroll, Lewis. *Alice's Adventures in Wonderland*. Illustrated by John Tenniel. Macmillan, (1865) 1963.

Chase, Alice Elizabeth. *Looking at Art*. Crowell, 1966.

Cleary, Beverly. *Dear Mr. Henshaw*. Morrow, 1983.

Cole, Joanna. *A New Treasury of Children's Poetry: Old Favorites and New Discoveries*. Doubleday, 1984.

Courlander, Harold. "The Wedding of the Hawk." *The King's Drum and Other African Stories*. Harcourt Brace Jovanovich, 1962.

Craft, Ruth. *Pieter Brueghel's The Fair*. Lippincott, 1975.

Crofut, William. *The Moon on the One Hand: Poetry in Song*. Atheneum, 1975.

Curtain Raiser Books. *Aida*. Illustrated by Helmut Luckman. Watts, 1970.

Curtain Raiser Books. *The Flying Dutchman*. Illustrated by Helmut Luckman. Watts, 1969.

Curtain Raiser Books. *The Magic Flute*. Illustrated by Riera Rojas. Watts, 1970.

D'Amato, Janet, and Alex D'Amato. *African Crafts You Can Make*. Messner, 1969.

Dayrell, Elphinstone. *Why the Sun and the Moon Live in the Sky*. Illustrated by Blair Lent. Houghton Mifflin, 1968.

Duncan, Lois. *Chapters: My Growth as a Writer*. Little, Brown, 1982.

Evans, Mark. *Scott Joplin and the Ragtime Years*. Dodd, Mead, 1976.

Farnay, Josie, and Claude Soleillant. *Egypt: Activities and Projects in Color*. Sterling, 1978.

Fine, Joan. *I Carve Stone*. Photos by David Anderson. Crowell, 1979.

Fleischman, Paul. *I Am Phoenix: Poems for Two Voices*. Illustrated by Ken Nutt. Harper and Row, 1985.

Forbes, Esther. *Johnny Tremain*. Houghton Mifflin, 1943.

Gardam, Jane. *A Long Way from Verona*. Macmillan, 1971.

Glubok, Shirley. *Art of Colonial America*. Macmillan, 1970.

Glubok, Shirley. *Doll's Houses: Life in Miniature*. Harper and Row, 1984.

Glubok, Shirley. *The Art of Egypt under the Pharaohs*. Macmillan, 1980.

Goffstein, M.B. *An Artist*. Harper and Row, 1980.

Goodall, John. *The Story of an English Village*. Atheneum, 1979.

Grahame, Kenneth. *The Wind in the Willows*. Illustrated by Ernest H. Shepard. Scribners, 1908.

Grimm, Jakob, and Wilhelm Grimm. *Hansel and Gretel*. Illustrated by Susan Jeffers. Dial, 1980.

Grimm, Jakob, and Wilhelm Grimm. *Hansel and Gretel*. Retold by Rika Lesser. Illustrated by Paul O. Zelinsky. Dodd, Mead, 1984.

Grimm, Jakob, and Wilhelm Grimm. *Hansel and Gretel*. Translated by Elizabeth D. Crawford. Illustrated by Lisbeth Zwerger. Morrow, 1979.

Grimm, Jakob, and Wilhelm Grimm. *Hansel and Gretel*. Illustrated by Adrienne Adams. Scribner, 1975.

Grimm, Jakob, and Wilhelm Grimm. *Hansel and Gretel*. Illustrated by Paul Galdone. McGraw-Hill, 1982.

Hodges, Walter C. *Shakespeare's Theatre*. Coward-McCann, 1964; Putnam, 1980.

Isadora, Rachel. *Opening Night*. Greenwillow, 1984.

Kerr, M.E. *Me! Me! Me! Me! Me!: Not a Novel*. Harper and Row, 1983.

Kinney, Jean, and Cle Kinney. *23 Varieties of Ethnic Art and How to Make Each One*. Atheneum, 1976.

Kuskin, Karla. *The Philharmonic Gets Dressed*. Illustrated by Marc Simont. Harper and Row, 1982.

Lewis, Brenda Ralph. *Famous Names in Music: Bach to Britten*. Wayland, 1979.

Lewis, Robert. *Advice to Players*. Harper and Row, 1980.

Low, Alice. *The Macmillan Book of Greek Gods and*

Heroes. Macmillan, 1985.

Lowndes, Rosemary, and Claude Kailer. *Make Your Own World of the Theater.* Little, Brown, 1982.

Meigs, Cornelia. *Invincible Louisa.* Little, 1933.

Moss, Anita, and Jon C. Stott (Eds.). *The Family of Stories: An Anthology of Children's Literature.* Holt, Rinehart and Winston, 1986.

Pettit, Florence H. *How to Make Whirligigs and Whimmy Diddles and Other American Folkcraft Objects.* Crowell, 1972.

Powers, Bill. *Behind the Scenes of a Broadway Musical.* Crown, 1982.

Quackenbush, Robert. *Stage Door to Terror.* Prentice-Hall, 1985.

Raboff, Ernest. *Marc Chagall.* Ernest Benn (London), 1980.

Raboff, Ernest. *Paul Klee.* Ernest Benn (London), 1980.

Raboff, Ernest. *Pierre-Auguste Renoir.* Ernest Benn (London), 1980.

Ross, Tony. *The Three Pigs.* Pantheon, 1983.

Sadler, Catherine Edwards (Reteller). *Heaven's Reward: Fairy Tales from China.* Atheneum, 1985.

Stevenson, Robert Louis. *A Child's Garden of Verses.* Illustrated by Jesse Willcox Smith. Scribner's, 1885.

Travers, Pamela L. *Mary Poppins.* Harcourt Brace Jovanovich, 1981.

Uchida, Yoshiko. "Momotaro: Boy-of-the-Peach." *The Dancing Kettle and Other Japanese Folk Tales.* Harcourt Brace Jovanovich, 1949. (Also in *The Arbuthnot Anthology of Children's Literature,* fourth edition, revised by Zena Sutherland. Scott, Foresman, 1976.)

Ure, Mary. *Supermouse.* Morrow, 1984.

Vuong, Lynette Dyer. *The Brocaded Slipper and Other Vietnamese Tales.* Addison Wesley, 1982.

Wildsmith, Brian. *Give a Dog a Bone.* Pantheon, 1985.

Willson, Robina Beckles. *The Voice of Music.* Atheneum, 1976.

Zola, Meguido. *Karin Kain: Born to Dance.* Grolier, 1983.

Teaching Higher Order Reading Skills with Literature: Intermediate Grades

Lee Galda

Inferring Character Traits

- Book: *The Great Gilly Hopkins* by Katherine Paterson (Crowell, 1978)

- This activity is designed to help students recognize character traits and relationships among characters. They will also recognize changes in those traits and relationships as the book progresses. The activity can be used appropriately with any book that has well-developed main characters.

  SAY: Who is the main character?
  DO: Write that name in the center of a large piece of paper. (You'll want to save this, so don't use the chalkboard.)
  SAY: What is he or she like? Tell me about him or her.
  DO: Write descriptors under the name, then draw a box around the name and all descriptors.
  SAY: Who else is important in the story?
  DO: Write their names evenly spaced around the center box.
  SAY: How does the main character feel about them?
  DO: Write responses on arrows running away from the center box toward each other box.
  SAY: How does each minor character feel about the main character?
  DO: Write responses on arrows running from the outer boxes toward the center box. The result will resemble this:

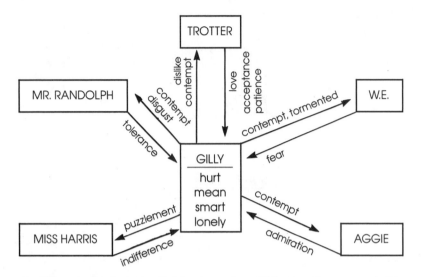

- After students have finished reading *Gilly Hopkins,* repeat this procedure, considering only the final six chapters. When the second chart is completed, compare it to the first, discussing the changes in Gilly's character and her attitudes toward others. After you have used this strategy with the group, individuals can apply it to other books they read.

  This also can be expanded into a close study of Paterson's character development if you ask students to find examples from the text to justify their answers. You can trace the change in Gilly chapter by chapter. This activity can be expanded by adding traits for each of the minor characters mentioned.

Based on an idea by A. Butler and J. Turbill, *Towards a Reading—Writing Classroom,* PETA (Heinemann), 1984.

Recognizing Story Structure

Teaching Idea

- Book: *The Napping House* by Audrey Wood. Illustrated by Don Wood (Harcourt Brace Jovanovich, 1984)
- This activity is designed to help children recognize various kinds of story structures. The example in this activity is a cumulative tale. Other graphic forms may be designed to suit other stories. The circle story for *Where the Wild Things Are* on pages 56-57 would be one such graphic form.

- Begin by reading the story.

  SAY: What happens or what character appears first?

  DO: Write the answer in a small box in the center left of a board or chart.

  SAY: Then what happens or who appears?

  DO: Write the answer in a slightly larger box to the right of the first one. Repeat process until climax, then begin to draw smaller boxes. The result will look something like this:

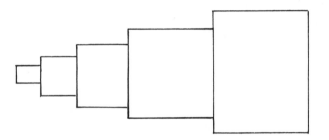

- Other graphic forms may be devised to suit other structures. For example, a cumulative tale might be displayed in this manner:

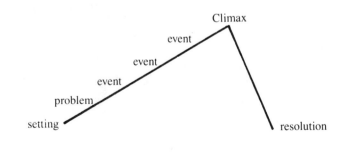

You might also want to experiment with using classical story structure labels such as setting, problem, event, climax, conclusion, or resolution using this form.

Inferring Comparisons

- Books: Any three variants of any folktale, such as *Cinderella* by Charles Perrault, retold by Amy Ehrlich, and illustrated by Susan Jeffers (Dial, 1985); *Yeh-Shen* by Ai-ling Louie and illustrated by Ed Young (Philomel, 1982); and *Cinderella* by Grimm, illustrated by Svend Otto S. (Larousse, 1978)
- This activity is designed to help children infer similarities and differences in literature. Although it is especially easy to do with folktales, other literature also can be used. For example, three pieces of realistic fiction that treat the same theme in different ways might be compared. This activity works well with elementary and middle school students.
- On chart paper, list down the left margin the dimensions along which you wish to compare the books. Then across the top write the title and author or illustrator of each book and label additional columns "Similarities," "Differences," and "Conclusions." If, for example, your first category is setting, you might:

    SAY: What is the setting of the first story? Where does the story take place?
    DO: Write answers in the appropriate space. Repeat the process for versions two and three. Then compare the three settings.
    SAY: How are these settings alike?
    DO: Write answers in the appropriate space.
    SAY: How are these settings different?
    DO: Write answers.

*From **Cinderella** retold by Amy Ehrlich, pictures by Susan Jeffers. Pictures copyright © 1985 by Susan Jeffers. Reproduced by permission of the publisher, Dial Books for Young Readers.*

SAY: What conclusions can we draw from this information?

DO: Write answers. Repeat this procedure for each story feature you have decided to discuss. The result will resemble this:

	Perraut/Jeffers Cinderella	Grimm/ Svend Otto S. Cinderella	Louie/Young Yeh-Shen	Similarities	Differences	Conclusions
Setting	"Once"–long ago when there were palaces.	Long ago when there were palaces.	In the dim past in Southern China.	All happened long ago.	Yeh-Shen takes place in China, all others in Europe.	Story comes from long ago and different places.
Characters	Beautiful Cinderella, father, stepmother, 2 stepsisters, prince, fairy godmother.	Beautiful Cinderella, father, stepmother, 2 stepsisters, prince.	Beautiful Yeh-Shen, stepmother, stepsister.	Main character has stepmother and 1 or 2 step-sisters and is always beautiful.	Yeh-Shen's father is dead. Has only one stepsister.	Main characters' real mothers are dead. All have stepmothers.
Problem	Cinderella mistreated, had to do all the work, not allowed to attend ball.	Cinderella mistreated, had to do all heavy work, not allowed to go to ball.	Yeh-Shen had to do heaviest, most unpleasant chores. Step-mother kills pet fish. Yeh-Shen can't go to festival.	All main charac-ters are mis-treated. All are not allowed to go somewhere special.	Yeh-Shen goes to a festival, not a ball.	Stepmother hates main character because she is beautiful.
Magic	Fairy godmother waves her wand and turns pump-kin into coach, mice into horses, rats into coach-men, rags into gown, and gives Cinderella a pair of glass slippers.	Birds help do her work and hazel tree on mother's grave gives her ball gowns.	The bones of her dead fish give her dress, and warn her not to lose shoes.	All have magic which gives main character beau-tiful clothes.	One has fairy godmother, one a magic tree, one a magic fish.	Magic varies according to story but all have some kind of magic.
Events	Cinderella goes to ball twice, loses slipper by accident. Prince finds slipper.	Cinderella goes to ball 3 times. Prince puts tar on stairs and slipper sticks. Prince finds slipper.	Yeh-Shen goes to festival once, loses shoe by accident, returns home. King is given slipper, searches for owner.	All main charac-ters go where they want to go and all lose slipper. Slippers are all small.	One loses slipper because king tricks her. One goes out once, one twice, one three times.	Losing the slipper is important to story.
Ending	Cinderella puts on lost slipper, god-mother turns rags into gown, for-gives sisters, marries prince, marries sisters to lords of the court.	Sisters mutlilate feet to fit slip-per, Cinderella puts on lost slipper and rides off to marry prince. Doves peck out stepsisters' eyes.	Yeh-Shen takes slipper from king who follows her. When she puts both on her rags become gown. Marries king. Stepmother and sister are later crushed to death by stones.	All are married to noblemen when their little feet fit slipper.	One forgives and rewards sisters, birds punish sisters in one, nature punishes in one.	Good is rewarded.

Based on ideas by Linda Western, "A Comparative Study of Literature through Folk Tale Variants," *Language Arts*, 1980, *57*, 395-402, and Bernice Cullinan, *Literature and the Child*, Harcourt Brace Jovanovich, 1981, 176; 178-179.

Distinguishing between Fact and Opinion/ Verifying Authenticity

Teaching Idea

- Books: *Popcorn* by Millicent Selsam, illustrated by Jerome Wexler (Morrow, 1976) and *The Popcorn Book* by Tomie dePaola (Holiday House, 1978)

- This activity helps children notice opinions versus facts, when there are discrepancies in facts, and how to verify the authenticity of the information presented in a book. This activity would work well with informational books on a variety of topics. It is also appropriate to use with historical fiction and biography. See, for example, some of the biographies of heroes of the American Revolution by Jean Fritz and compare her well-researched books with those by other authors. Another activity might involve a comparison of information found in reference books with information found in nonfiction trade books. For more details, see Bernice Cullinan, *Literature and the Child*, Harcourt Brace Jovanovich, 1981, pp. 347-351.

*Illustration from **The Popcorn Book** copyright © 1978 by Tomie dePaola. Used by permission of Holiday House.*

DO: Read aloud dePaola's *The Popcorn Book*.

SAY: What facts have we learned about popcorn from this book?

DO: List answers on the board.

SAY: How do we know these are facts?

DO: Discuss how one character reads facts from the encyclopedia and how the encyclopedia language is in print different from that of the character's dialogue. Put question marks after any items from your list that turn out to be questionable.

SAY: Why does the author know so much about popcorn?

DO: Discuss the fact that "eat(ing) a lot of popcorn" and consulting an encyclopedia do not make dePaola an expert. Then read through page 13 of Selsam's *Popcorn*.

SAY: What facts have we learned about popcorn from this book?

DO: List answers on the board.

SAY: How do we know these are facts?

DO: Discuss with the class how Selsam is careful to distinguish between fact and opinion with words such as "possibly" and "think" versus "know" and "for sure." Put question marks after items on your list that turn out to be questionable.

SAY: Are there any differences in the facts we've learned from each book? (There are.) Are there any conflicting facts? (There are.)

SAY: Why does this author know so much about popcorn?

DO: Discuss Selsam's credentials (which are considerable and are listed on the back flap of the jacket).

SAY: Which author's information about popcorn do you think would be the most trustworthy? Why? How can we check to see who is right?

DO: Send students to other sources, including encyclopedias, to verify facts. Finish with a discussion comparing all of the sources and summarizing general principles.

Galda

Recognizing the Characteristics of a Genre

- Book: *Aesop's Fables,* illustrated by Heide Holder (Viking, 1981)
- This activity is designed to help children recognize the characteristics that distinguish one genre from another. It can be adapted for many grades and genres. Chapter 7 by Strickland discusses ways for elementary students to study myths, legends, and mysteries. The activity on inferring comparisons of the Cinderella stories on pages 92-93 also can be amended to focus on characteristics of fairy tales by comparing different fairy tales rather than different variants of the same tale. The procedures presented here focus on fables.
- Over a period of several days, read aloud a variety of fables. Have fables available for independent reading. Then, announce a "Favorite Fable" day on which students may retell their favorite fable. After students have finished their retellings, do the following.

> SAY: These stories are all fables because they all are alike in some ways. What is one thing you notice about all of the stories we have heard?
>
> DO: Write answers on board as they're given. Essential points are that they are short and dramatic, the characters are animals or inanimate objects that portray human characteristics, and there is an explicitly stated moral at the end.
>
> SAY: Most fables were written a long time ago, but some authors write modern fables. Here's a book of fables written by a modern author. Let's see if the characteristics of fables that we've noticed will hold true for these modern stories.
>
> DO: Read aloud Arnold Lobel's *Fables* (Harper & Row, 1980). Then discuss their similarity to older fables. Finish the discussion with a reminder of the characteristics of the genre and invite your class to create a class book of modern fables. You might want to do one together first. One good way to begin is to think of a moral, like "never put off until tomorrow what you can do today," and then create a story to illustrate it.

The following books could help to extend this activity.

Aesop. *The Fables of Aesop: 143 Moral Tales Retold.* Selected and edited by Ruth Spriggs. Illustrated by Frank Barber. Rand-McNally, 1976.

Aesop. *Aesop's Fables.* Selected and illustrated by Michael Hague. Holt, Rinehart, and Winston, 1985.

Bennett, Charles H. *Bennett's Fables: From Aesop and Others Translated into Human Nature.* Viking, 1978.

Brown, Marcia. *Once a Mouse.* Scribner's 1961.

Section 4
Children's Literature in the Upper Grades

In the upper grades (6 to 8), readers often strike out on their own in independent reading and become enchanted with a favorite genre. Dianne Monson provides a wealth of ideas for working with students who prefer realistic fiction and historical fiction. She shows how to focus on characterization and point of view for students at three different levels of literary understanding. Jean Greenlaw and Margaret McIntosh present a theoretical framework for creative thinking; they anchor it in practice by selecting science fiction and fantasy to develop aspects of higher level reading and thinking.

Chapter 9
Characterization in Literature: Realistic and Historical Fiction

Dianne Monson

In the upper elementary grades, students should begin to have both affective and intellectual interactions with literature. Teachers are challenged to create units that hold students' interest and, at the same time, encourage them to recognize some of the literary qualities of well-written fiction. Success depends on the choice of literature and on the way it is presented. For that reason, unit planning demands that teachers be knowledgeable about literature and about the responses students are likely to make when they read.

The most important and basic response to a story involves the emotions. Rosenblatt (1969) calls attention to literary experience as a transaction in which readers bring to bear on interpretation of the text a whole set of understandings from their lives, giving to the text as well as receiving from it, and in that way

constructing meaning from the story. A story that evokes laughter, wonder, sadness, curiosity, or fear invites a reader to have a genuine interaction with characters and the events in their lives.

When students are captivated by the characters or actions in a story, they often have vivid memories of the story that can serve later as a basis for judging other stories. For example, students often become emotionally involved with a character like Julie in *Julie of the Wolves* (George). Later, when they read another novel in which a protagonist faces similar problems, they may compare that character to Julie and feel that Julie seems more or less real or interesting than the character in the second book.

When reflection on a book reaches this level, the reader has let an emotional response lead to a more intellectual judgment about the literary quality of the story. If the reader also realizes that Jean George excels in describing characters and settings and uses them to her advantage in her portrayal of Julie, the reader is giving some evidence of knowledge about critical elements of literature.

Emotional responses may also lead readers to recognize that they share some of the fears and hopes of a story character like Julie. They may think about the way Julie tries to bridge two cultures. That may lead them to think about other children who face similar kinds of conflicts because they have moved from one country to another. In that way, interpretation extends a story so readers recognize that some of its elements apply to situations close to their own lives.

In addition to emotional/personal responses and interpretations of the meaning of the story, the common responses to literature are awareness of literary elements and critical judgment of the quality of a story or the behavior of a character. All of these will be discussed in this chapter.

Unit Planning

Characterization Unit

Generally, units can be organized to emphasize specific authors, works, or elements of stories such as theme, characterization, setting, or plot. They can focus on one book or several books.

Virtually all fiction revolves around some sort of conflict that involves a major character, so the plot may be built around the person's struggle to deal with the problem. The source of conflict may be one person against another, an individual against society, people against nature, or idea against idea. In some

books there is more than one source of conflict. *Julie of the Wolves* (George) shows conflict of a person against nature as Julie strives to survive in the harsh Arctic tundra. It also shows the conflict of a person against society as she seeks to find her identity, whether as a member of the Eskimo society or of the competing white culture.

If the central concern of a book is with characterization, it is important to examine the ways in which the author chooses to develop the character. Is description the major technique? Does the author make effective use of dialogue to reveal personal qualities of the characters? Are other subtle ways used to let readers know what sort of person a story character is? Does the person change throughout the course of the story? If so, what are the indications of change? These and other questions guide the selection of activities for the unit that follows. Underlying it all is the desire to create a unit that draws readers into the story and encourages them to bring their life experiences to their reading.

Realistic and Historical Fiction Unit

This unit is constructed in three stages. The first is based on the observation that many upper elementary students have had little, if any, experience with formal response to literature. If that is true for your students, begin at stage one with a series of class sessions devoted to a book that all students read at the same time or that you read aloud. If your students are more advanced, you may want to begin with the second stage, in which students read independently from a choice of contemporary realistic or historical fiction titles. The third stage is an enrichment section, building on study of characterization and other elements introduced with contemporary fiction but extending the study to include historical fiction.

Stage One

Patricia MacLachlan's *Sarah, Plain and Tall* is a good choice for a unit introduction because it is well written and short enough to read aloud in one long session or in two shorter ones. The book, which appeals to students of virtually any age, is the story of a motherless pioneer family. The story has many facets. Begin by calling attention to the fact that these are likable people, each with the strength to bear a kind of burden. This emphasis on personal qualities is most appealing to students, though they also find the descriptions of setting interesting. In order to help students respond personally to a story, introduce the unit by posing this situation for them: Suppose you are trying to write a description of someone interesting and you want to know more about that person. What questions would you ask? Have children work together to create a list of questions. Once such a list has been created, it can serve as a resource for listening to the character descriptions in

*Jacket illustration from **Sarah Plain and Tall** by Patricia Mac-Lachlan, jacket by Marcia Sewall. Copyright © 1985 by Patricia MacLachlan, jacket art copyright © 1985 by Marcia Sewall, jacket © 1985 by Harper & Row, Publishers. Reprinted by permission.*

Getting to Know a Character in a Book

Pose this problem for students: Suppose you want to know more about a person so you can write a description of him or her. What questions would you ask the person?

Let students work in small groups to generate questions. The following are some of the possibilities they may suggest:

- Describe yourself. What do you look like? What do you like best about the way you look? What would you like to change about your looks?
- What is your favorite color? What are your favorite clothes? What color don't you like? Why?
- What do you like to do best when nobody else is around? Do you collect anything? Do you have a favorite book? What kinds of jobs do you dislike the most at school? At home?
- Who are your best friends? Why do you like them? Who don't you like? Why?
- How do you feel about brothers and sisters? Do you get along with yours? When you disagree, what is it usually about? Do you like them better as you are getting older?
- If you could go anywhere you choose, where would it be? Why?
- If you could plan one whole day for yourself, what would you do?

After children have created such a list, they can use it as a resource in getting to know characters in books, pretending to ask the questions of the book character and trying to imagine what the character would answer.

Sarah, Plain and Tall. Ask children to listen as you read and try to determine what the author reveals about Sarah and the other three people in the story. Which of their questions can they answer after hearing the story?

The text is not only short, but it is as spare as the language of people in Sarah's native Maine. Children may need some guidance if they are to uncover elements of Sarah's character. You may want to reread her letters to the family so children notice the way Sarah tells them something about herself even before they meet. Her postscript in the first letter–"Do you have opinions on cats? I have one."–is important because it suggests that she loves animals, or at least cats. The tone seems to indicate that she is willing to ask whether Papa has opinions about cats, but she would probably not leave hers behind. She also describes herself as strong, hard working, and willing to travel. She tells Anna that she can braid hair and make stew, but that she would rather build bookshelves and paint.

In order to help students grasp Sarah's personal characteristics, have them refer to the list of questions cited earlier. Recall Sarah's descriptions of Maine and the ocean, her love for the colors of the sea, and the sea shells that she brought with her to remind her of home. Notice her love for animals. Sarah reveals her enjoyment of the outdoors when

Characterization in Literature

she takes the children with her to swim in the horse pond. Her thoughtfulness and fondness for the children are evident in many ways.

Other characters are less clearly developed, for the focus is on Sarah. However, Caleb is shown as a wistful child, wanting to hear over again what he was like as a baby, wishing Anna could remember their mother's songs and sing them to him, and worrying that Sarah won't like them well enough to stay. Anna is the narrator, so we have to learn about her from what she chooses to tell. She tells us some things about Papa that reveal his feelings about Sarah. He picks flowers for her hair, makes a dune out of straw for her to slide on so she won't miss her sand dunes, and brings her the first roses of summer. Papa changes from a sad, lonely man to a man who can smile again.

Point of View

Students can learn about character interpretation by retelling a story from one character's point of view. In *Sarah, Plain and Tall*, the story is told through Anna's eyes. Yet, the other people involved must have had their own perceptions of the events. Encourage students to retell the story as Papa, Caleb, or Sarah might tell it. It is a good challenge to try to see the prairie and the family as Sarah might have observed them as she arrived at the farm the first time. Some readers might be able to infer Papa's concerns about his motherless family and his thoughts as he wrote his advertisement for the newspapers. Encourage students to write what Papa might have said in the advertisement.

The conflict in this book is essentially geographic. Sarah is separated from the sea she loves. The contrasts between the prairie and the sea are presented in a number of ways. The colors, terrain, flowers, and wildlife of both are clearly described. Students can make lists of attributes of the sea and of the prairie. Using that information, ask them to choose scenes from the book to illustrate the farm or Sarah's home in Maine. To plan the illustrations, ask students to decide on the content of the pictures and to consider whether they would use colors and, if so, which colors.

Compare the setting and situation in this book with those in *Dakota Dugout* (Turner) and *Prairie Songs* (Conrad).

Stage Two

Following the reading and discussion of *Sarah, Plain and Tall*, give students a choice of contemporary novels that offer readers opportunities to experience the lives of others who bear burdens and have dreams. Some that work well for character analysis are *The Eighteenth Emergency, Good-Bye, Chicken Little, The Great Gilly Hopkins, Julie of the Wolves, One-Eyed Cat, Sea Glass,* and *The Summer of the Swans*.

The following brief response guides suggest some ways to help students recognize the development of a character. Remind students that an author can show what a character is like through journals, letters, dialogues, descriptions, first person statements, and comments made by the narrator.

The Eighteenth Emergency (Byars). When Benjie (Mouse) is threatened by Marv Hammerman, the sixth grade bully, he falls back on an old game he and his friend Ezzie used to play—how to survive life's greatest emergencies. List as many of Mouse's "emergencies" as you can remember and tell how the boys planned to deal with them. How

Observing Character Traits

There are several strategies for helping students record character traits.
- Have them answer as many of the questions as they can from the lists they made earlier and use the answers to write a brief biography of one character.
- Another more concrete strategy is to have students chart the most evident qualities of each character. An example follows.

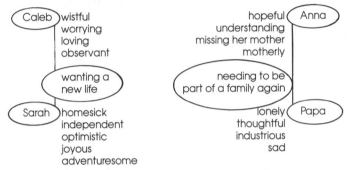

Caleb — wistful, worrying, loving, observant

wanting a new life

Sarah — homesick, independent, optimistic, joyous, adventuresome

hopeful, understanding, missing her mother, motherly — Anna

needing to be part of a family again

lonely, thoughtful, industrious, sad — Papa

Drawing semicircles around pairs of characters shows some of the ways these people are alike (Flender, 1985). Students may think of other descriptive words and phrases to use in their charts. In a useful modification of this chart, you can leave room beside or below each adjective for students to briefly include the evidence from the story that gives a basis for including the word. For example, readers can tell that Sarah is homesick for the sea because she sometimes listens to the shells she brought along with her and often speaks of her love for the colors of the sea. She even buys colored pencils so those colors can be re-created. Students could draw a seashell and a set of colored pencils to add that evidence.

does Mouse plan to survive emergency encounters with Hammerman? What happens instead? Do you agree that Mouse comes out a winner? Why? Why not? What words or phrases would you use to describe Mouse's looks, behavior, and feelings at the beginning of the story? At the end?

Good-Bye, Chicken Little (Byars). What caused Jimmy to be so afraid that he began to call himself Chicken Little? How does he react to his uncle's death? What finally helps him overcome his fears? Do you admire

Jimmy or feel sorry for him? Do your feelings change as the story develops?

The Great Gilly Hopkins (Paterson). Gilly seems able to cope with a succession of foster homes because she decides she can stand anything as long as she is in charge. Look for clues that Gilly, for all her toughness, isn't sure who has gotten rid of whom each time she moves out of a foster home. Notice, too, all the indications Gilly gives that show she really wants to live with her mother. As the story moves along, pay attention to signs that

Gilly may be mellowing. Compare your feelings about Gilly at the beginning of the story with the way you feel about her at the conclusion. What words or phrases best describe Gilly's looks, behavior, and feelings?

Julie of the Wolves (George). As you are reading or after you have finished, make a chart of the way Julie/Miyax behaves and thinks in each of her lives, as a girl living in the Eskimo culture and as a girl living in the white culture. You might organize it this way:

	Julie	Miyax
Dangers		
Behavior		
Dress		
Fears		
Happiness		
Other		

In addition, you may want to illustrate her home territory in both Alaska and San Francisco. The author ends the story without letting us know what Miyax and Kapugen might say to one another at the conclusion. Write your own conversation. If you are interested in the descriptions of wolf behavior in this book, do some research about their habits and compare that information with what is given here.

One-Eyed Cat (Fox). As you read, think about these questions: Why did the one-eyed cat haunt Ned? When he thought Mr. Scully had lost interest in the cat, why did Ned say he was afraid he'd have to carry the cat alone and it seemed to weigh 200 pounds? What do you think Ned's father would have told him if he had confessed his fears about blinding the cat? What adjectives or phrases would you use to describe each of the major characters: Ned, Mama, Papa, Uncle Hilary, Mrs. Scallop, Mr. Scully?

Sea Glass (Yep). This story is told in first person by the main character. Study the way Craig's character is described through his comments about himself, his relationship with his father, and his problems with other kids. Notice how Kenyon changes as she drops her facade and reveals her feelings when she talks with Craig alone, behind Uncle's place. Think about how the author lets you know that it is important to accept yourself as you are and not try to be someone you aren't. What words or phrases best describe Craig's looks, behavior, and feelings?

The Summer of the Swans (Byars). As you read the first description of Charlie, how did you picture him? How old? Were you surprised when you learned his real age? Record some descriptions of Charlie that show his dependence on Sara and the loneliness he experiences when he is out of her sight. Consider Sara as a character. As you read, collect anecdotes that reveal her feelings about herself. A good beginning is the episode where she describes herself. Jot down some evidence from the story that lets you know what her relationship is to Charlie and take note of the change in Sara throughout the story. What words or phrases would you use to describe her at the beginning of the story? At the end?

Taking the Role of a Character

In order to encourage affective response, have students write a list of five things they like to do and five things they don't like to do. Then have them respond to the same assignment as though they were a character in the book they just read. It is best not to have these lists shared, but do ask students to think about whether they are like or are different from the characters in the novels.

A related activity involves readers in the

*Illustration from **Julie of the Wolves** by Jean Craighead George. Text copyright © 1972 by Jean Craighead George, illustrations copyright © 1972 by John Schoenherr. Harper and Row, Publishers, Inc. Reprinted by permission.*

role of a best friend who is called upon to give advice to the story character. As introduction, ask students whether they could be a best friend to the main character in the story they chose to read. Why? Why not? Have they had any of the experiences the person had, any experiences they could pass along that might help the person? To set this in motion, tell each student, "You are the best friend of a character in one of the books you have recently read. Identify an episode that caused that character unhappiness or concern." (Some likely ones are Ned's distress when he first sees the one-eyed cat or Sara's concern when she realizes that Charlie is missing.) What might you say to that person to help him or her deal with the situation?

Interpretation of fiction calls for making inferences about the characters' feelings, the possible effects of an event on the lives of people involved, or the way an event in a story is related to something similar to what the reader has experienced. In order to help readers make inferences about the thoughts of story characters, pose this question: If a main character in the book you just finished were to write a letter to Sarah (in *Sarah, Plain and Tall*) and, in the letter, point out some ways their lives are alike, what would the person say? What questions might he or she ask of Sarah, Caleb, Anna, or Papa? Write the letter.

Another strategy for exploring characterization is to assign students to small groups, with each child representing a different book. Ask each one to introduce his or her main character, describing some physical characteristics as well as some information about the problems the person faced. If they wish, they might include illustrations of the characters. Next, have students tell what the character might say in response to these questions: If you were going to tell someone about yourself, what would you say? Do you think your problem is worse than the problems of the other people represented here? Why? Why not?

In order to encourage students to evaluate some aspect of the book, ask them which character they like better, Sarah or a main character from the contemporary books they read. Why? Are the contemporary characters in those books like her in any way?

Stage Three

Reading and studying historical fiction is a natural extension in a unit focused on realistic fiction. Characters in both types of books share the same universal feelings—hope, love, hate, fear, joy. Both genres reveal personal, social, or political conflicts. Furthermore, reading historical fiction allows students to recognize the importance of an author's treatment of time and place and the description of a story setting.

A third stage of this unit might be the choice of one of several books with historical settings. If you want the whole group to read the same book, *Johnny Tremain* (Forbes) would be a natural choice. It is a good novel and interests most students. The growth in Johnny as a person from beginning to ending of the story is striking. The treatment of the Revolutionary War period in American history is accurate and so are references to the people who were influential in creating the new government.

Offer students a choice of books to read: *My Brother Sam Is Dead* (Collier and Collier) is a good book to pair with *Johnny Tremain*. It presents a picture of Revolutionary War times through the eyes of a family torn by divided loyalties. The parents are loyal to King George while the older brother fights with the patriots. Whereas *Johnny Tremain* is mainly urban, *My Brother Sam Is Dead* has a rural setting. The two provide material for interesting comparisons.

Offer students a choice of books that deal with problems encountered by people who settled in the United States in different time periods. *The Sign of the Beaver* (Speare), *Dragonwings* (Yep), and *Journey to Topaz* (Uchida) are an effective combination. The first book is set in the 1700s and portrays relationships between settlers and Indians. The second book explores the conditions faced by Chinese laborers living in San Francisco at the turn of the century, seen through the eyes of a boy who comes from China to join his father in America. The third book portrays the prejudice shown to people of Japanese descent when they were sent to relocation camps during World War II.

In each of these books, a major character struggles with conflict produced by difficulties with people and with nature. The activities that follow are suggested to help students recognize the qualities of major characters in the books they choose. They are appropriate to use with historical fiction selections as well as with contemporary books suggested in Stage Two of the unit. Attention to literary elements of the books included in the unit can highlight characterization, plot, and setting.

Characterization

Encourage students to think about the following questions as they read: What does the author let us know about the main character? What clues to personality are given? Using those clues, what words might be used on a characterization chart like the one done for *Sarah, Plain and Tall*?

One activity students particularly enjoy is the TV talk show. Here, one student is the interviewer and two or three others represent characters from the books they have read during the unit. In order to make the characters seem more real, students are encouraged to wear or carry some object that relates to the theme of the story. For example, in one classroom, two girls chose to be interviewed as Sara from *The Summer of the Swans* and Gilly from *The Great Gilly Hopkins*.

*Jacket illustration by Lynd Ward from **Johnny Tremain** by Esther Forbes. Copyright © 1943 by Esther Forbes Hoskins. Copyright © renewed 1971 by Linwood M. Erskine, Jr., Executor of the Estate. Reprinted by permission of Houghton Mifflin Company.*

Characterization in Literature

Sara wore very large, laceup tennis shoes that accented the size of her feet. Gilly wore unkempt clothes, had messy hair, and chewed bubble gum, blowing her famous bubbles from time to time. Some of the questions they answered included: When did you begin to realize that people don't like you very well? Does that bother you? What do you think is your best quality? What do you think is your worst quality? If you could do anything you wanted, what would it be? Who would you most like to surprise? Who means the most to you? The activity can be adapted for characters from historical fiction. (See Monson & McClenathan, 1979, pp. 100-104.)

Writing activities can give students opportunities to interact with story characters. While students are reading a novel, have them keep journal entries that a major character might have written. The entries need not cover the entire book, but should highlight events of most importance to that character. This experience of trying to write from the point of view of a story character helps students enter into the life of the person, trying to think as the character might think about events that occur.

Readers Theatre (described in chapter 8), with its emphasis on oral interpretation, is another way to encourage readers to determine what kind of person a story character really is. It is particularly important because dialogue is one of the most effective means an author has for developing characterization. Students should be reminded of that at the beginning of the activity.

Select a short episode that is fairly self-contained. There should be several characters in addition to the narrator. The key is to choose selections from books written with fine dialogue style. Although the dialogue should be left untouched, it is sometimes necessary to shorten the narrative passages. Once the selection has been scripted, students can choose their parts. It is important that they have read the entire book, or at least enough of it to recognize the personal qualities of the characters they are representing. With that background, let them think about how they

Students conducted a talk show similar to those on television. One was interviewed as Sara from **The Summer of the Swans** *and one as Gilly from* **The Great Gilly Hopkins.**

would describe the characters and then decide how the characters would speak.

Readers Theatre can be informal. No sets or costumes are used and dramatic actions are limited to facial expressions and some gestures. Dramatic effect is achieved by interaction among the readers. They should stand in a semicircle so they can all make eye contact when they want to reinforce the relationships among characters. Since the narrator is a key person, that part should be read by a good reader.

An enjoyable exercise that calls for creative thinking about a story character's likes and dislikes is described by Rodriguez and Badaczewski (1978, p. 62). They suggest presenting students with this problem: You are the garbage collector who visits ____'s house on your regular route. As you have come to know the people on your route, you have found that their garbage is a good indication of their personalities, likes, and dislikes. Describe the types of garbage you are likely to find at ____'s house and what that garbage reveals about ____. The assignment can be varied by asking students to pose as the clerk at a local grocery store the character might visit.

Plot

What is the source of conflict in this book? Does it stem from conflict between people? People against nature? People against society? Idea against idea? How does the main character deal with the conflict? In order to prepare students to think about the way conflict is handled, have each one write a sentence on a separate strip of paper for each kind of conflict the main character is involved in and another sentence for the way the person tries to resolve the conflict. Put students into groups where several different books are represented. Encourage them to look for cases where characters from different books are involved in similar kinds of conflicts and to consider which character seems more successful in dealing with the problem. As follow-up, the sentence strips can be used to produce a display or a mobile showing common types of conflicts/resolutions in realistic fiction.

Setting

Ask students to think back to *Sarah, Plain and Tall*. Have them find evidence that the book does not have a contemporary setting (travel by horse and buggy, horses to pull the plow, a mail order bride). Then ask, could the story take place now? Encourage students to present arguments for or against that proposition.

Following the discussion of the setting for *Sarah, Plain and Tall,* ask students to write information from the description of setting for their contemporary novel. What evidence can they find that allows them to identify the time the story takes place and its location? Is it rural, urban, small town? Could they illustrate a jacket cover that would give a good sense of time and place?

A sense of time and place also can be explored when students have read novels from different decades or periods in history. In this case, let them assume the identity of characters from the novels and discuss an issue as each character might see it (Cline & McBride, 1983). Some issues that provoke good discussion are whether children ought to take responsibility for helping out with work around the house or whether twelve year olds should be given the freedom to stay out alone past 10:00 p.m. The contrast in answers from Sarah in *Sarah, Plain and Tall,* Julie in *Julie of the Wolves,* Gilly in *The Great Gilly*

Hopkins, and Sara in *The Summer of the Swans* makes an interesting discussion.

Conclusion

The activities described here can help you achieve several goals in teaching a literature unit. First, and perhaps most important, they help students become emotionally involved with the major characters. Some of the activities build on an emotional engagement to involve students intellectually as well, inviting them to notice techniques good authors use to create believable, well-rounded characters. As students consider the kinds of conflict faced by people in contemporary and historical fiction, they can become aware of times when they have had to deal with similar problems. Recognizing concerns that unite people of all ages and all times is one step toward recognizing universal themes that permeate all good literature. Finally, you will enrich your reading program by using material that engages the hearts as well as the minds of your students.

References
Cline, Ruth, and McBride, William. *A guide to literature for young adults.* Chicago: Scott, Foresman, 1983.

Flender, Mary G. Charting book discussions: A method of presenting literature in the elementary grades. *Children's literature in education,* 1985, *16,* 84-92.

Monson, Dianne, and McClenathan, DayAnn (Eds.). *Developing active readers: Ideas for parents, teachers, and librarians.* Newark, DE: International Reading Association, 1979.

Rodriguez, Raymond J., and Badaczewski, Dennis. *A guidebook for teaching literature.* Newton, MA: Allyn and Bacon, 1978.

Rosenblatt, Louise M. *Literature as exploration,* revised edition. New York: Noble, 1969.

Children's Books
Byars, Betsy. *The Eighteenth Emergency.* Viking, 1973.

Byars, Betsy. *Good-Bye, Chicken Little.* Harper and Row, 1979.

Byars, Betsy. *The Summer of the Swans.* Viking, 1970.

Collier, James Lincoln, and Christopher Collier. *My Brother Sam Is Dead.* Four Winds, 1974.

Conrad, Pam. *Prairie Songs.* Harper and Row, 1985.

Forbes, Esther. *Johnny Tremain.* Houghton Mifflin, 1943.

Fox, Paula. *One-Eyed Cat.* Bradbury, 1984.

George, Jean. *Julie of the Wolves.* Harper, 1972.

MacLachlan, Patricia. *Sarah, Plain and Tall.* Charlotte Zolotow Book. Harper and Row, 1985.

Paterson, Katherine. *The Great Gilly Hopkins.* Crowell, 1978.

Speare, Elizabeth George. *The Sign of the Beaver.* Houghton Mifflin, 1983.

Turner, Ann. *Dakota Dugout.* Illustrated by Ronald Himler. Macmillan, 1985.

Uchida, Yoshiko. *Journey to Topaz.* Margaret McElderry Book. Scribner, 1971.

Yep, Laurence. *Dragonwings.* Harper and Row, 1975.

Yep, Laurence. *Sea Glass.* Harper and Row, 1979.

Chapter 10
Science Fiction and Fantasy Worth Teaching to Teens

M. Jean Greenlaw
Margaret E. McIntosh

Recently, we conducted a twelve week class on high fantasy in a junior high school and on the last day asked the students to make any comments they had about the class or what they had learned. Several students responded with specific bits of information, and then Chris piped up, "You took the bore out of reading!" We accepted this as the ultimate compliment; it was a reflection of the teaching techniques and the wonderful books we had used for the course. We present here many of the teaching ideas we used and we have expanded them to include science fiction as well as high fantasy.

Science fiction and fantasy are literature of the imagination. Imagination can take us anywhere and help us adapt to any circumstance. In *The Language of the Night,* Ursula LeGuin (1979, p. 44) comments:

> I believe that all the best faculties of a mature human being exist in the child, and that if these faculties are encouraged in youth they will act well and wisely in the adult, but if they are repressed and denied in the child they will stunt and cripple the adult personality. And finally, I believe that one of the most deeply human, and humane, of these faculties is the power of imagination; so that it is our pleasant duty, as librarians, or teachers, or parents, or writers, or simply as grownups, to encourage that faculty of imagination in our children, to encourage it to grow freely, by giving it the best, absolutely the best and purest nourishment that it can absorb.

It is not enough merely to suggest good books to students; they have to be guided in strategies that will give them the knowledge and skill to explore books on their own. One framework we find useful is Frank E. Williams's model (Williams, 1970), which provides a means to enhance the cognitive and affective processes involved in creativity and productivity. Williams listed the features of creative thinking; we provide a definition for the eighteen points of this model and give an example that reflects the content of three high fantasy series: The Chronicles of Prydain by Lloyd Alexander, The Dark Is Rising series by Susan Cooper and The Earthsea Trilogy by Ursula K. LeGuin. These same strategies can be used with any science fiction or fantasy book.

Williams's Model

Paradox. A seemingly contradictory statement that may nonetheless be true. *Example:* The character Eilonwy, in The Chronicles of Prydain, seems to be scatterbrained, but generally produces the most sensible suggestions to solve a predicament.

Attribute. A quality or characteristic belonging to a person or thing; a distinctive feature. *Example:* The character Ged, in The Earthsea Trilogy, is impetuous and self-centered at the beginning of the series and reasonable and selfless at the end.

Analogy. A form of logical inference, based on a correspondence in some respect between people or things otherwise dissimilar. *Example:* High fantasy is to Welsh Mabinogian as a Greek play is to mythology.

Discrepancy. A divergence or disagreement, as between facts or claims; inconsistency. *Example:* The strings on Fflewddur Fflam's harp break whenever he "stretches the truth."

Provocative questions. Questions intended to excite and stimulate students' thinking and exploration of new ideas. *Example:* Ged never punishes or rewards. Is this hard to live with? Why or why not?

Examples of change. A demonstration of how dynamic the world is or can be; making provisions for activities that employ modifications or substitutions. *Example:* Will, a character in The Dark Is Rising series, alternates attributes in various situations. At times he is an Old One, and at other times, an eleven year old.

Examples of habit. Habits are a constant, often unconscious inclination to perform some act, acquired through frequent repetition; activities for this strategy seek to provide examples that encourage students to avoid habit bound thinking. *Example:* Merriman, a character in The Dark Is Rising series, accepts the fact that children are able to perform heroic tasks to pursue a quest.

Organized random search. Developing a structure to lead randomly to another structure. *Example:* Taran in The Chronicles of Prydain, Will in The Dark Is Rising series, and Ged in The Earthsea Trilogy all search for an understanding of their destiny in a seemingly random way.

Skills of search. The development of methods for searching for information; this might include trial and error, historical, experimental, etc. *Example:* Students can be asked to discover the relationship among the Welsh Mabinogian, The Chronicles of Prydain, and The Dark Is Rising series.

Tolerance for ambiguity. Ambiguous situations are open to multiple interpretations; activities for this strategy present open-ended situations for discussion. *Example:* The Walker, in The Dark Is Rising series, was used by the Old Ones. Was he fairly treated in his punishment?

Intuitive expression. Intuition is the act of knowing without the use of rational processes; activities for this strategy seek to encourage making guesses based on hunches or emotions. *Example:* Taran's ultimate destiny is not revealed until the conclusion of the five books. Foreshadowing is used to provide hints

Greenlaw and McIntosh

which can enable students to predict his destiny at the end of each book.

Adjustment to development. This strategy seeks to enable students to develop or change rather than to merely adjust to situations. *Example:* How does Bran, who is different, develop his own persona rather than responding to what others think of him?

Study creative people and processes. Activities for this strategy encourage students to look at people who are creative and explore the processes they use. *Example:* Students can study the essays of Lloyd Alexander to determine what they reveal about him and his fantasy books.

Evaluate situations. Activities for this strategy encourage students to engage in prediction from the delineation of actions and ideas and to form conclusions based on careful consideration of consequences and inferences. *Example:* Predict whether Tenar, a character in *The Tombs of Atuan,* will give up being the Eaten One and go with Ged, or remain as the Priestess of the Tombs.

Creative reading skill. Using text as a stimulus for the creation of an idea or a product. *Example:* Create a banner that represents yourself as the banners in The Chronicles of Prydain represent the characters.

Creative listening skill. Encouraging students to respond to oral text in ways that will allow them to develop ideas and respond to questions. *Example:* Have students listen to selections read with differing intonations and ask them to delineate the differences in interpretations.

Creative writing skill. Encouraging students to express their feelings and emotions in clearly written passages. *Example:* Have students make regular entries in a journal to record their responses to the author's work as well as responses to questions such as "Who would you trust enough to give your name to, as Ged did in The Earthsea Trilogy?"

Visualization skill. Activities for this strategy encourage students to form a mental image that includes an unusual perspective. *Example:* Have students produce a dragon in some creative form.

Science Fiction

The nature of science fiction allows for development of thematic categories. The following discussion explores seven categories, including specific activities for each category. Each activity reflects one of the points from Williams's model and can be presented to the students in the form of a worksheet. It would be possible to work with several reading groups, each reading in a different thematic area, or the whole class could pursue several of the themes.

THEME: Search for Other Worlds. There is a fascination with the possibility that humans could inhabit other worlds and with life in other worlds. The following books explore these topics: *An Alien Music* (Johnson and Johnson), *Calling B for Butterfly* (Lawrence), *Earthseed* (Sargeant) and *The Stars Will Speak* (Zebrowski).

ACTIVITY: Attributes. It has become apparent that Earth is reaching its capacity to support human life. The decision has been made to send ships into space to search for new worlds to inhabit. Prepare a list of the attributes necessary for a world that could be inhabited by humans or a list of the attributes necessary for the humans who would make this journey.

THEME: Conflict of Cultures. Differences often cause misunderstandings. Science fiction authors often pursue this concept by exploring an alien society, while at the same time their stories reflect the same tendencies on earth. Some books using this theme are *The Delikon* (Hoover), *Devil on My Back* (Hughes), *Dreamsnake* (McIntyre), *Moon-Flash* (McKillip), and *The Moon and the Face* (McKillip).

ACTIVITY: Adjustment to development. Conflict between cultures and attempts to bridge their differences are themes often explored in science fiction. In *The Delikon,* an alien race has ruled Earth for many years, and the humans are finally rebelling. Varina, an alien, is talking to Aaron, one of her former pupils, about why he is rebelling (p. 60):

> "But I want to understand why."
> He studied her face; then he shook his head again. "I don't think you can, Varina. I don't think we can ever understand each other. Your intelligence is different in a way I cannot grasp...your ...concept of rationality so vast that it seems simple or naive to me. As if your people cannot grasp the effect they have on us. There is an unbridgeable gulf...."

In the book you have chosen, describe the conflict between cultures and how the protagonist develops or changes as a response to this conflict. Also, describe a conflict of cultures in the real world and tell how one might develop or change because of it.

THEME: The Potential of Science. Pure science is value free. It is the responsibility of those who use scientific discoveries to determine to use them for good or evil. Cloning and genetic manipulation are but two controversial topics in science today. Books with this theme include *Anna to the Infinite Power* (Ames), *Caught in the Organ Draft* (Asimov), and *Joshua Son of None* (Freedman).

ACTIVITY: Discrepancy. Science and technology have enhanced the quality of life for many. However, a discrepancy exists because science and technology have also brought us to the edge of disaster. Isaac Asimov, in *Caught in the Organ Draft* (p. x), writes:

> Is it not terrible, then, that our gathered knowledge, put to the service of our passions, has brought us to the edge of self-destruction? And if we destroy ourselves, is it not plain that we destroy something that may be utterly unique in the universe and that may never be replaced? Should we not labor to keep ourselves and our civilization alive out of self-love and vanity, if no nobler emotion will do?

Choose one category of science or technology and explore its benefits and its harmful aspects. Is there a balance?

THEME: Mind Control. Mental telepathy, ESP, and control of others through the power of the mind have always intrigued readers of science fiction. Fear of loss of self-control is balanced by the lure of the possibility of communicating with others across time and space. Some books dealing with this theme are *Out of Sight, Out of Mind* (Aaron), *Mind-Call* (Belden), *Worldstone* (Strauss), and *Psion* (Vinge).

ACTIVITY: Visualization. Mind control and mental telepathy are often explored in science fiction. The conflict is often expressed as the protagonist's struggle for self control or a struggle between the protagonist and an outside force for the protagonist's mind. In *Mind-Call* (p. 237), Tallie masters self control.

> Tallie did for herself what she had once done for Bree: she accepted and conquered her past. She wrenched her mental door off its hinges and poured out all the dammed-up words and images. As they vanished, Tallie knew that, at last, she was well. Never again would she accept other visualizations as her own.

Greenlaw and McIntosh

After reading one of the books on mind control, visualize a situation in which someone has control of your mind. Describe the situation and how you would regain control.

THEME: Search for Eternal Life. What would it be like to live forever? Science fiction writers often share their visions of this phenomenon through stories that tell its good and bad sides. Some books with this theme are *Earthchild, Earth Song, Ram Song* (all by Webb) and *Welcome, Chaos* (Wilhelm).

ACTIVITY: Provocative question. Would you be willing to turn to science to find the secret to eternal life? What would be the consequence of living forever? Would you tire of your life? Share the consequences described in the book you selected and respond to their implications. Then delineate several consequences or benefits you imagine would accompany eternal life.

THEME: Nuclear Power. Older science fiction books tend to emphasize the potential of nuclear power, while newer books often emphasize its destructive possibilities. Books with this theme include *Out of Time* (Chambers), *The Danger Quotient* (Johnson and Johnson), *Children of the Dust* (Lawrence), *Wolf of Shadows* (Strieber), and *Brother in the Land* (Swindells).

ACTIVITY: Skills of search. Nuclear power is of concern to all segments of society. Books have probed such topics as nuclear holocaust, nuclear winter, and nuclear waste disposal. Select one novel that explores such a topic and compare the fictional treatment to at least three informational sources. Try to locate differing opinions in your informational selections.

THEME: Probing Sequels and Series. When we discover an intriguing character or setting in a book, we often wish the story wouldn't end or that the author would give us more as soon as possible. Science fiction writers often oblige us. For example, Douglas Hill with *Galactic Warlord, Deathwing over Veynaa, Day of the Starwind, Planet of the Warlord,* and *Young Legionary;* Anne McCaffrey with *Dragonsong, Dragonsinger,* and *Dragondrums;* and Frederik Pohl et al. with *The Great Science Fiction Series.*

ACTIVITIES: Attributes, intuitive expression, studying creative people and processes. Some authors create a character or world for a book or short story and then realize the character or world will not let them go; they must continue the story through sequels. Choose an author who has written in this fashion, then read several of the books or short stories and try to delineate the attributes of the character or world that compelled the author to continue the story. Then try to locate an essay by the author describing his or her writing. Is the author's explanation similar to your intuitive reasoning? In what ways?

High Fantasy

High fantasy is characterized by a secondary world setting, an "Everyman" protagonist, strong characterization, a quest, the struggle between good and evil, value laden events and ideas, and an overriding theme concerned with basic human relations and attitudes. Fantasy portrays a world that includes supernatural elements or nonrational phenomena. Paradoxically, good fantasy uses these elements to put readers more closely in touch with reality. Ursula LeGuin (1979, p. 44) says that fantasy is truth–not factual, but true.

"Fantasy's truth challenges, even threatens all that is false, all that is phony, unnecessary, and trivial in life." Fantasy expresses reality in a way that realistic fiction cannot, through the language of the inner self.

Because high fantasy appeals to the inner self, it is an ideal genre to stimulate creative responses. The following teaching ideas are designed to elicit creative responses from students. Each set of activities is based on a high fantasy book or series.

The Chronicles of Prydain. This five book high fantasy series, set in the land of Prydain, depicts Taran's quest to discover his destiny. As he grows to manhood he faces many adventures with the help of his companions:

Fflewddur Fflam, a spiky haired, not so truthful bard; Eilonwy, a princess in waiting whose pithy comments add sparkle to the series; and Gurgi, a "poor tender-headed" creature who looks like an "owl's nest in need of housecleaning." The five books by Lloyd Alexander are *The Book of Three*, *The Black Cauldron*, *The Castle of Llyr*, *Taran Wanderer*, and *The High King*.

ACTIVITY: Discrepancy. People often view themselves differently from the way others see them. An example is Gast the Generous. In *Taran Wanderer*, after hearing Gast call himself "the Generous," Taran says, "I think he'd make a miser seem a prodigal in com-

*Illustration from **The High King** by Lloyd Alexander, illustration by Evaline Ness. Copyright © 1968 by Lloyd Alexander. Holt, Rinehart and Winston. Reprinted by permission.*

parison." Make a list of some discrepant names for characters in The Chronicles of Prydain. For example, Fflewddur the Truthteller.

ACTIVITY: Paradox, tolerance for ambiguity. Develop an answer to the following: "Which character in The Chronicles of Prydain is the most paradoxical?" Remember that a paradox is a seemingly contradictory statement that may nonetheless be true. Although it may be true in fact, it does not seem to be so. Jot down your answer, along with a few supporting statements, and include the page number and name of the book. When you are finished, meet with three other students to reach a consensus regarding which character is most paradoxical.

ACTIVITY: Analogy, creative reading. In The Chronicles of Prydain, the various kings proclaim their presence by displaying their royal banners. These banners represent each king's character traits. For example, King Smoit is represented by a bear. List some of your character traits, then represent them metaphorically. When you are satisfied with your idea, make your own banner.

The Earthsea Trilogy. Ursula LeGuin combines all the elements of high fantasy in her stories about Ged, a young wizard who has a destiny far beyond the one he imagines for himself. Ged grows and matures as he confronts first himself and then other representations of good and evil. The three books are *Wizard of Earthsea*, *The Tombs of Atuan*, and *The Farthest Shore*.

ACTIVITY: Examples of change.

Illusion fools the beholder's senses; it makes him see and hear and feel that the thing is changed. But it does not change the thing. To change this rock into a jewel, you must change its true name. And to do that, my son, even to so small a scrap of the world, is to change the world. It can be done...but you must not change one thing, one pebble, one grain of sand, until you know what good and evil will follow on that act" (*A Wizard of Earthsea*, pp. 43-44).

Choose one common object and decide how you would change it. What would be the consequences of changing it? List or describe them. Then, knowing what the consequences would be, what circumstances would cause you to change the object anyway? Describe the situation.

ACTIVITY: Attributes—provocative question. "Who knows a man's name holds that man's life in his keeping." Throughout The Earthsea Trilogy, it is clear that one does not give someone else one's name without a great deal of consideration and thought. If, in our world, those who know your name held power over you, to whom would you tell your name? What attributes do these people share that make them trustworthy enough to know your name?

The Riddlemaster of Hed. Like The Earthsea Trilogy, this series is for seasoned high fantasy readers. Morgon, land ruler of Hed, has a more difficult role than simply caring for Hed. He must battle "The High One" for his own life and the life of every person in his country. The books are *The Riddle-Master of Hed*, *Heir of Sea and Fire*, and *Harpist in the Wind* by Patricia A. McKillip.

ACTIVITY: Attributes. Morgon is capable of changing his shape. In order to assume the shape of an object, he must truly understand the attributes of that object. In this passage he learns to assume the shape of a vesta:

He felt himself rooted, locked into the rhythms of the mountain; his own rhythms drained away from him, lost beyond memory in the silence that shaped him. Wordless knowledge moved through him, of slow measureless age, of fierce winds borne beyond the breaking point, of seasons beginning, ending, of a patient, unhurried waiting for something that lay deeper than roots, that lay sleeping in the earth deeper than the core of Isig, something on the verge of waking (*The Riddlemaster of Hed,* pp. 208-209).

Imagine that you are a master shape changer and that you teach others to change shape by telling them the attributes of the object they want to become. List objects of nature with each one's most inherent attribute.

ACTIVITY: Evaluate situations.

"Where will you go?"

"Into the forest, up a mountain–anywhere, as long as it's not here."

"I'm coming," Lyra said.

"No, absolutely–"

"The guard can stay here in the city, in case they are needed. But I am coming with you. It's a matter of honor."

Morgon looked at her silently, his eyes narrowed. She met them calmly. "What did you do?" he asked. "Did you take a vow?"

"No, I don't take vows. I make decisions."

(*Harpist in the Wind,* p. 102-103)

Would you rather have someone guarding you who had vowed to protect you or someone who had decided to protect you? Explain your decision and justify it with examples.

ACTIVITY: Evaluate situations. Throughout the series about the Riddlemaster of Hed, the notion of "land-rule" is referred to repeatedly. As you read, note any references to land-rule. Jot down page numbers and quotes. Formulate a theory as to what constitutes the land-rule and how it is passed from one person to another. Revise your theory as you gather additional information. Compare your final idea with those of others who have read these books.

The Kingdom of Damar series will eventually include more than the two books written to date. Both *The Hero and the Crown* and *The Blue Sword* by Robin McKinley are set in Damar, a mythical kingdom, but the stories take place generations apart.

ACTIVITY: Creative listening.

Harry asked Luthe, "Can you hear everything I'm thinking?"

"No," he replied. "Only those arrow-like thoughts that come flying out with particular violence. You have a better organized mind than most. Most people are distressing to talk to because they have no control over their thinking at all, and it is a constant barrage, like being attacked by a tangle of thornbushes, or having a large litter of kittens walking up your legs, hooking in their claws at every step. It's perhaps also an effective preventative to having one's mind read, for who can identify the individual thorn?" (*The Blue Sword,* p. 180).

Listen to the conversations of people around you for the next few days. In particular, listen for verbal evidence that a person has a well-organized mind (like Harry) or a disorganized mind that produces conversation that attacks like a thornbush. Record your evidence.

The Children of Ynell series chronicles the plight and ultimate triumph of the Seers of Ere–those special people who have extraordinary powers coveted and feared by those who do not have the same abilities. The books by Shirley Rousseau Murphy are *The Ring of Fire, The Wolf Bell, The Castle of Hope, Caves of Fire and Ice,* and *The Joining of the Stone.*

ACTIVITY: Creative writing. Ram wondered whether he had been born for the sole purpose of bringing the stone out of Ere.

> Fawdref...made Ram understand that no man was born to one thing. That there was no power that could make a babe come into the world for any purpose. There was only the coming together of powers and events, the linking into a whole that made time and need bring an urgency upon life. This was how he was born, a culmination to that urgency. There was no one intelligence that could dictate his birth or would presume to (*The Wolf Bell*, p. 86).

Write a thoughtful, cohesive response to the ideas expressed. You may agree, disagree, or wonder. Share your written response with another member of the class.

ACTIVITY: Visualization.

> Zephy strained to see or to feel with some sense what lay ahead and around them, but she could not; there was only the heavy blackness as if she could remember nothing else, did not know what light was....If you lived in darkness all your life, she thought, and had never seen light, you would not be able to imagine what the world looked like. Do we, Zephy, wondered, live in a world where there is something we can't see, but is there around us just the same? (*The Ring of Fire*, p. 105).

Visualize a parallel world that is going on around us but that we can't see. Describe it and describe how it can exist.

The Darkangel series by Meredith Ann Pierce will eventually include more than two books. It is a compelling fantasy set on the moon. It tells of a vampyre and the woman who loves him and saves him. The two books completed are *The Darkangel* and *A Gathering of Gargoyles.*

ACTIVITY: Visualization.

> "My people make such cloaks," the little man said. "We cannot bear the light of Solstar, for the Ancients made us to dwell underground. We may travel by night, or course, without difficulty, but when we must go overland by day, we must wear a daycloak....The fiber is such, and the weave is such–an ancient art, and one I regret I never learned–as to make the wearer unseen by day, for it is invisible to the light of Solstar (*A Gathering of Gargoyles*, p. 210-211).

Visualize a daycloak. Create a way to demonstrate the properties of such a garment.

Tolkien (1980, p. 120) states that children's books, "like their clothes, should allow for growth, and their books at any rate, should encourage it." Imaginative literature, including science fiction and fantasy, encourages growth in young readers. The books are not written to blatantly reveal their ultimate secrets; they are elusively suggestive (Cullinan, 1981). Great science fiction and fantasy writers have the ability to express truths and judgments too subtle for the intellect alone to comprehend, but readers may subconsciously absorb the ideas into their inner beings (Cameron, 1962).

Lloyd Alexander (1968), one of the greatest writers of imaginative literature, states:

> Children may not understand all that's happening below the surface of the story. It doesn't matter. Because even though they may not be able to define or verbalize it, they sense there's something more than meets the eye; on an almost subliminal level, they're aware of a richness of texture, of meaning and emotion–a richness that, in a great book, is inexhaustible. And the child may well come back to it again and again, perhaps long after he's stopped being a child.

Imaginative literature provides more opportunities for growth in reading and in self than any other type. Children and young adults should not only be allowed to read in this genre, but invited to. The ideas suggested herein are a means for you to invite and entice students into imaginative literature. It will enhance your reading program.

References

Alexander, Lloyd. *The alchemical experience.* Paper presented at the National Council of Teachers of English Conference, Milwaukee, 1968.

Cameron, Eleanor. *The green and burning tree: On the writing and enjoyment of children's books.* Boston: Little, Brown, 1962.

Cullinan, Bernice E., Karrer, Mary K., and Pillar, Arlene M. *Literature and the child.* New York: Harcourt Brace Jovanovich, 1981.

LeGuin, Ursula K. *The language of the night.* New York: Putnam, 1979.

Tolkien, J.R.R. Children and fairy stories. In Sheila Egoff, G.T. Stubbs, and L.F. Ashley (Eds.), *Only connect: Readings on children's literature.* Toronto: Oxford University Press, 1980, 111-120.

Williams, Frank E. *Classroom ideas for encouraging thinking and feeling,* second edition. Buffalo: D.O.K., 1970.

Children's Books

Aaron, Chester. *Out of Sight, Out of Mind.* Harper and Row, 1985.

Alexander, Lloyd. *The Black Cauldron.* Holt, Rinehart and Winston, 1966.

Alexander, Lloyd. *The Book of Three.* Holt, Rinehart and Winston, 1964.

Alexander, Lloyd. *The Castle of Llyr.* Holt, Rinehart and Winston, 1966.

Alexander, Lloyd. *The High King.* Holt, Rinehart and Winston, 1968.

Alexander, Lloyd. *Taran Wanderer.* Holt, Rinehart and Winston, 1967.

Ames, Mildred. *Anna to the Infinite Power.* Scribner's, 1981.

Asimov, Isaac (Ed.). *Caught in the Organ Draft.* Farrar, Straus and Giroux, 1983.

Belden, Wilanne. *Mind-Call.* Atheneum, 1981.

Chambers, Aidan (Ed.). *Out of Time.* Harper and Row, 1985.

Cooper, Susan. *The Dark Is Rising.* Atheneum, 1973.

Freedman, Nancy. *Joshua Son of None.* Delacorte, 1973.

Hill, Douglas. *Day of the Starwind.* Atheneum, 1981.

Hill, Douglas. *Deathwing over Veynaa.* Atheneum, 1981.

Hill, Douglas. *Galactic Warlord.* Atheneum, 1980.

Hill, Douglas. *Planet of the Warlord.* Atheneum, 1981.

Hill, Douglas. *Young Legionary.* Atheneum, 1983.

Hoover, H.M. *The Delikon.* Viking, 1977.

Hughes, Monica. *Devil on My Back.* Atheneum, 1985.

Johnson, Annabel, and Edgar Johnson. *An Alien Music.* Four Winds, 1982.

Johnson, Annabel, and Edgar Johnson. *The Danger Quotient.* Harper and Row, 1984.

Lawrence, Louise. *Calling B for Butterfly.* Harper and Row, 1982.

Lawrence, Louise. *Children of the Dust.* Harper and Row, 1985.

LeGuin, Ursula. *The Farthest Shore.* Atheneum, 1972.

LeGuin, Ursula. *The Tombs of Atuan.* Atheneum, 1970.

LeGuin, Ursula. *Wizard of Earthsea.* Parnassus, 1968.

McCaffrey, Anne. *Dragondrums.* Atheneum, 1979.

McCaffrey, Anne. *Dragonsinger.* Atheneum, 1977.

McCaffrey, Anne. *Dragonsong.* Atheneum, 1976.

McIntyre, Vonda. *Dreamsnake.* Houghton Mifflin, 1978.

McKillip, Patricia A. *Harpist in the Wind.* Atheneum, 1979.

McKillip, Patricia A. *Heir of Sea and Fire.* Atheneum, 1977.

McKillip, Patricia A. *The Riddle-Master of Hed.* Atheneum, 1976.

McKillip, Patricia A. *Moon-Flash.* Atheneum, 1984.

McKillip, Patricia A. *The Moon and the Face.* Atheneum, 1985.

McKinley, Robin. *The Blue Sword.* Greenwillow, 1982.

McKinley, Robin. *The Hero and the Crown.* Greenwillow, 1985.

Murphy, Shirley Rousseau. *The Castle of Hope.* Atheneum, 1980.

Murphy, Shirley Rousseau. *Caves of Fire and Ice.* Atheneum, 1980.

Murphy, Shirley Rousseau. *The Joining of the Stone.* Atheneum, 1981.

Murphy, Shirley Rousseau. *The Ring of Fire.* Atheneum, 1977.

Murphy, Shirley Rousseau. *The Wolf Bell.* Atheneum, 1979.

Pierce, Meredith Ann. *The Darkangel.* Little, Brown, 1982.

Pierce, Meredith Ann. *A Gathering of Gargoyles.* Little, Brown, 1984.

Pohl, Frederik et al. (Eds.). *The Great Science Fiction Series: Stories from the Best of the Science Fiction Series from 1944 to 1980 by 20 All-Time Favorite Writers.* Harper and Row, 1980.

Sargeant, Pamela. *Earthseed.* Harper and Row, 1983.

Strauss, Victoria. *Worldstone.* Four Winds Press, 1985.

Strieber, Whitley. *Wolf of Shadows.* Knopf, 1985.

Swindells, Robert. *Brother in the Land.* Holiday House, 1985.

Vinge, Joan. *Psion.* Delacorte, 1982.

Webb, Sharon. *Earth Song.* Atheneum, 1983.

Webb, Sharon. *Earthchild.* Atheneum, 1982.

Webb, Sharon. *Ram Song.* Atheneum, 1984.

Wilhelm, Kate. *Welcome, Chaos.* Houghton Mifflin, 1985.

Zebrowski, George. *The Stars Will Speak.* Harper and Row, 1985.

Teaching Higher Order Reading Skills with Literature: Upper Grades

Lee Galda

Attending to Details and Emotional Responses to Plot or Theme

Teaching Idea

- Book: *The Dark Is Rising* by Susan Cooper (Atheneum, 1973)
- This activity is designed to help students "unpack" a complex story. When used with a book such as *The Dark Is Rising,* it helps students recognize how setting works to further the action. It also helps them understand the complex unity of character and action that develops and maintains theme.
- You might approach this activity in at least two ways. You might have your students read the book on their own, or you could read the book aloud, pausing after each chapter. After allowing time for general response, do the following.

SAY: Where was the action taking place? (There are four settings; they are plotted below, with page numbers.)

DO: Write responses on *large* paper, noting page numbers and leaving plenty of space for additions.

SAY: What are the characteristics of this setting?

DO: List the students' responses on a separate sheet. Repeat this process for two or three chapters, or until your students are familiar with the procedure. You can then either continue to do this with the whole class, if you are reading aloud, or ask students to do it themselves if they are reading on their own.

When the book is completed, you will have a map which will resemble this:

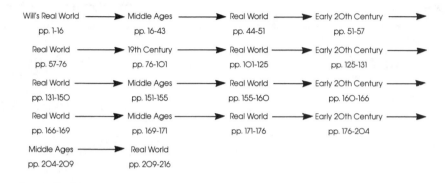

Will's Real World ⟶ Middle Ages ⟶ Real World ⟶ Early 20th Century ⟶
pp. 1-16   pp. 16-43   pp. 44-51   pp. 51-57

Real World ⟶ 19th Century ⟶ Real World ⟶ Early 20th Century ⟶
pp. 57-76   pp. 76-101   pp. 101-125   pp. 125-131

Real World ⟶ Middle Ages ⟶ Real World ⟶ Early 20th Century ⟶
pp. 131-150   pp. 151-155   pp. 155-160   pp. 160-166

Real World ⟶ Middle Ages ⟶ Real World ⟶ Early 20th Century ⟶
pp. 166-169   pp. 169-171   pp. 171-176   pp. 176-204

Middle Ages ⟶ Real World
pp. 204-209   pp. 209-216

This map will be accompanied by a sheet with descriptors of each setting generated by your students.

> DO: You can now break your class into groups and assign each a different task.
> 1. Look for clues that the setting is going to change, moving in and out of fantasy. (For example, the signs Will carries change temperature, music is heard, fire is present, etc.)
> 2. Describe Will as he is in the real world at the beginning of the story, using examples from the text to support your descriptions. Then do the same for Will as he is in the fantasy world. Compare them, looking for consistencies and differences. Describe Will again as he is at the end of the story.
> 3. Compare minor characters (like Merriman or the lady) in their real world and fantasy world guises.
> 4. Plot the major events of the story on the setting map.
> 5. Identify and explain some of the important symbols in the story (the Mandala, runes, Old Ones, the Dark).

Have each group present its findings to the whole class. It is helpful to record in brief form some of the information on the original map of the setting. The first entry will resemble the following:

Will's Real World
pp. 1-16
radio static
rabbits are afraid
rooks are strange
Farmer Dawson's warning and gift
the old man
snowstorm
rook's feather

Presentation and discussion of this information should lead to an extended discussion of how plot, setting, and character development are woven together to create a powerful story of the struggle between the forces of dark and the forces of light.

Other books with themes of good versus evil include *Over Sea, Under Stone, Greenwitch, The Grey King,* and *Silver on the Tree,* all by Susan Cooper (which complete the sequence in which *The Dark Is Rising* is the second volume); the Earthsea Trilogy by Ursula K. LeGuin; and *Darkangel* and *A Gathering of Gargoyles* by Meredith Ann Pierce. LeGuin and Pierce write for audiences a bit more sophisticated than the audience for which the Cooper sequence is intended.

Section 5
Children's Literature in Broader Contexts

Teachers using children's literature in the reading program need support from teacher educators, reading clinicians, administrators, and librarians. Ira Aaron presents a carefully executed plan for combining children's literature with other classroom materials, suggesting specific children's books and showing how they can be integrated into a basic reading program. Roselmina Indrisano and Jean Paratore show how they use children's literature in a reading clinic with disabled readers. They focus on concept literacy and pattern literacy–two areas of learning known to be helpful in fostering competent readers. Francie Alexander describes the guidelines and framework for the California Reading Initiative, one state's response to the growing demand for quality literature in reading programs. The comprehensive plan may serve as a model for other states. Arlene Pillar shows where to find new reading materials as you go beyond the titles cited in this book, providing an extensive, well ordered list of resources for teachers.

Chapter 11
Enriching the Basal Reading Program with Literature

Ira E. Aaron

The major aim of reading instruction programs is to develop readers who not only *can* read but who *do* read and who will continue to read throughout life. To accomplish this goal, children must have ample opportunities to read good literature. Certainly skills are important, but skills alone will not get the job done. They must be taught in a context that encourages students to read and to love reading.

As many as 85 to 90 percent of the elementary classrooms in the United States use basal reading series as core instructional materials. No basal series was ever intended to be a complete, self-contained reading program. The pupil texts of a series do not and cannot include as much reading material as students need. Teachers who supplement basals with a variety of other printed matter–newspapers, magazines, and many books from the library–are providing a rich environment for developing readers.

A pupil text may contain thirty-five short selections and maybe a few poems. A typical series at a first reader level will have about 220 pages, with almost half of them devoted to pictures. A second semester, third reader pupil text may contain 350 pages, with about one-third of the pages devoted to pictures or other illustrations. Though the pupil text contains a large amount of material to be read, it certainly does not include enough to meet the needs of children. Additional reading from children's literature gives students opportunities to practice the skills they have been taught–often in longer selections than those found in the pupil text.

The timeworn statement that "children learn to read by reading" would be more accurate if it were changed to "children's reading ability is maintained and enhanced by reading." Certainly, just reading without systematic instruction will not accomplish the task; children must be *taught* to read. However, in order to maintain proficiency in reading, students must use the skills they have learned. Extensive reading leads to increased vocabularies, enlarged knowledge, broadened interests, greater appreciation of writing techniques and styles, and improved speed of comprehension. Further, enjoyment and appreciation of good literature are increased by wide reading.

This chapter discusses ways children's books may be used in reading programs in which basal reader series are the core instructional materials. The books mentioned and the suggestions made should be equally appropriate for all reading teachers, regardless of the approaches they use.

Five broad areas of discussion follow: The first three deal with using selections in the pupil texts of basal series to motivate children to read related children's books; the remaining two areas deal with extending skills through reading trade books. The two skills clusters discussed–understanding, appreciating, and evaluating characters' feelings and actions and recognizing and appreciating different types of literature–are ways of using children's and young adults' books to increase students' skills while at the same time stressing the goal of enjoying reading. Other important skills cluster areas, such as understanding and appreciating writers' language, style, purpose, and techniques, are discussed in other chapters in this book.

Using Text Selections to Encourage Reading of Trade Books

Pupil texts of basal reader series often contain selections from the best writers of children's books. Why not use these selections as springboards for further reading of good literature? In addition, selections in basal reader texts suggest books that would be appropriate for teachers to read aloud to children. As using children's books along with basal series is discussed, each point is illustrated with specific book titles. Since in almost all instances, any one of dozens of titles could have been used as appropriate examples, titles should be thought of as illustrative of the many books available.

Use Selections in Pupil Texts to Encourage Students to Read the Book from Which a Selection Was Taken

Pupil texts of basal reader series frequently include exact reproductions, adaptations, or abridgements of chapters from children's books. Examples include excerpts from *Charlotte's Web* (White), *Queenie Peevy* (Burch), *Winnie the Pooh* (Milne), *Little House in the Big Woods* (Wilder), *The Summer of the Swans* (Byars), *Johnny Tremain* (Forbes), and *The Wind in the Willows* (Grahame). Using an excerpt sets the stage to encourage students to read the entire book from which the selection came. With the help of the librarian, multiple copies of the book may be collected for classroom use. Paperback editions are available for most books excerpted in basal series. Interested students may read the book independently. Occasionally, the teacher may prefer to use a book from which a part has been reprinted in the pupil text as a story to be read aloud, a chapter at a time, to an entire class.

Basal reader series are usually used in a school or school system for at least five years. Therefore, when a series is adopted, teachers and librarians should determine which children's books to order in quantity to use as follow up to selections in the pupil texts.

Use Selections in Pupil Texts to Introduce Students to Other Selections by the Same Writer

Pupil texts contain excerpts or reprints of some of the best writers of children's literature. Often the books excerpted are several years old before they appear in a pupil text. Part of the delay results from the time it takes to build a series of basal readers. Also, some writers and their publishers may be reluctant to grant reproduction rights on newly published materials.

A selection from a Beverly Cleary story in a pupil text will call attention to her other books such as *Ramona and Her Father; Ramona and Her Mother; Ramona Quimby, Age 8; Ramona Forever; Ralph S. Mouse; Lucky Chuck;* and *Dear Mr. Henshaw,* the 1984 Newbery Medal winner.

A Betsy Byars excerpt can be used to introduce other books by Byars such as *The Pinballs, The Cybil War, The Glory Girl, The Computer Nut, Cracker Jackson,* and *The Not-Just-Anybody Family.* A Robert Burch excerpt sets the stage for mentioning his *Queenie Peevy, Two That Were Tough, Ida Early Comes Over the Mountain,* and *Christmas with Ida Early.*

After the class reads a particular poem in a pupil text, teachers may wish to read aloud other poems by the same poet or to encourage students to read them on their own. The works of well-known poets often appear in pupil texts. *A Light in the Attic* and *Where the Sidewalk Ends* by Shel Silverstein are among the most popular collections of verse with readers of all ages. Myra Cohn Livingston's many volumes of poetry range from the an-

*Illustration from **Ramona Forever** by Beverly Cleary, illustrated by Alan Tiegreen. Illustrations copyright © 1984 William Morrow and Company, Inc. Reprinted by permission.*

thology *A Song I Sang to You* to *Sea Songs,* a collection of her own poetry. Jack Prelutsky's humorous verses appear in *The Random House Book of Poetry for Children, It's Snowing! It's Snowing!* and *My Parents Think I'm Sleeping.* Other poets whose works are often included in basal reader pupil texts are Robert Frost, Lee Bennett Hopkins, Langston Hughes, Karla Kuskin, Vachel Lindsay, David McCord, Eve Merriam, Aileen Fisher, Lilian Moore, John Ciardi, and Carl Sandburg. Be sure to give students room to enjoy poetry; too much analysis can kill interest in reading poetry and verse.

Encourage Students to Compare Selections in Pupil Texts with Original Sources

Fiction and informational selections in pupil texts are often exact reprints of the originals; in fact, poems are almost always reprinted with no change in the wording, though accompanying illustrations may differ from the originals. On the other hand, informational and fictional selections may be abridged or adapted for various reasons for inclusion in pupil texts. In abridgements, selections are shortened to fit available space, or wording may be changed to avoid sexist language, a possible ethnic slur, an ambiguous idea, or an outdated statement. When selections are cut to fit space restrictions, descriptions may be edited to require less space.

Selections also may be edited to fit an approximate reading grade level. Even though publishers exert considerable effort to avoid distorting the story or information and to assure comprehensible text, a given selection may be inadvertently changed in the adaptation.

Illustrations accompanying the printed text may differ from those used in the original book. Occasionally, pupil text illustrations may be included specifically to furnish information to increase comprehensibility of the text, whereas the original may have contained no illustrations.

Students should be encouraged to compare the pupil text version with that of the original and to raise questions about the logic or accuracy of part of a selection in a pupil text. One such comparison grew from a second grade child noticing that a book in the room library was the same story as a selection her group had just read in the pupil text. The book was Judy Blume's *The One in the Middle Is the Green Kangaroo.* The teacher suggested the group compare the pupil text version with the original book. In the pupil text version, students observed that some descriptive paragraphs had been deleted and a few words had been changed. They also noted that the illustrations were in color rather than black line drawings as in the original book. The children concluded that they liked the illustrations better in the pupil text but felt the original text was slightly better than the abridged version; the few extra paragraphs in the original made it a little easier to follow the story.

In activities of this sort, children gain some understandings of where selections in pupil texts come from and how they may be modified from their original versions. More important, though, such activities give students opportunities to make comparisons, thus increasing their ability to think critically. They also may enhance student appreciation of how a selection is written as well as how illustrators picture scenes from the stories. Comparing illustrations is a valid critical reading activity.

Illustration from **One-Eyed Cat** by Paula Fox. Copyright © 1984 by Paula Fox. Reproduced by permission of Bradbury Press, an affiliate of Macmillan, Inc.

Extending Reading Skills through Trade Books

Use Children's Books to Develop Understanding, Appreciation, and Evaluation of Characters' Feelings and Actions

One of the most important uses of trade books in the reading program is to provide students with opportunities to understand, appreciate, and evaluate the feelings and actions of characters. Though some attention is given to this area in pupil texts, not nearly enough reinforcement can come from the basal text selections alone. Identifying with a character, developing a feeling for or against him or her, leads to a deeper level of involvement and makes reading a book more enjoyable and meaningful. Hundreds of well-written trade books with easy to like–and sometimes easy to hate–characters are available. A few

books and their characters will be cited here as examples of the many available in most good school libraries.

The young teenage owner, or prospective owner, of a motorcycle will appreciate Beverly Cleary's *Lucky Chuck,* in which a worried mother, highway courtesy, and a police officer are among Chuck's concerns. The book, which begins by labeling the parts of a motorcycle, is very easy to read and, thus, would appeal to reluctant older readers.

In *One-Eyed Cat,* Paula Fox tells the story of eleven-year-old Ned's attempts to handle the guilt that grows from his belief that he blinded a stray cat in one eye when he fired a forbidden air rifle at a dark shadow in the night. To cover his attempts to care for the one eyed cat, he tells little lies that build up until Ned feels he is "perched on the top rung of a ladder built of lies; the ladder was leaning against nothing" (p. 189). The author describes in beautiful language Ned's feelings toward his minister father; his mother who is bedridden with rheumatoid arthritis; Mrs. Scallop, the talkative housekeeper; and Mr. Scully, a kind man for whom Ned performs odd jobs. Just reading the book–or listening to it read aloud–reinforces appreciation of the actions and feelings of the characters. Encourage students to contrast Ned's feelings toward the various characters in the book. Ned's guilt sets the stage for readers to evaluate his feelings and actions. Should he feel guilty, or is he overreacting? Why? Should he have used the air rifle? Why or why not?

Many books help students develop skill in understanding, appreciating, and evaluating feelings and actions of characters. Beverly Cleary's books about Ramona depict a growing girl facing various problems related to being a member of the Quimby family–and sometimes solving them in a humorous way. In *Ramona and Her Father,* Ramona must adjust to having an out-of-work father at home during the day. In *Ramona and Her Mother,* Ramona feels neglected because her mother works outside the home. In *Ramona Quimby, Age 8,* Ramona has to adapt to a working mother and a student father who now is studying to become an art teacher. In *Ramona Forever,* she faces the possibility of having to move and seeing her favorite aunt marry a man Ramona initially dislikes.

Cynthia Voigt's books about the Tillerman family offer contrasts in characters. Thirteen-year-old Dicey, ten-year-old James, nine-year-old Maybeth, and six-year-old Sammy, abandoned by their mentally ill mother in *Homecoming,* start out walking to find Aunt Cilla. After days of near starvation, the children reach Aunt Cilla's, only to learn that she died several months earlier. Following a brief stay with Aunt Cilla's daughter, the children

travel by bus, boat, and on foot to reach the Maryland farm of Abigail Tillerman, their grandmother whom they did not know existed until a few weeks earlier. *Dicey's Song* depicts the emotional strains the four children and their grandmother endure in getting to know and care about one another in this newfound relationship. Near the end of *Dicey's Song* as well as in *Homecoming,* the reader learns that "Uncle Bullet" was killed in Vietnam. *The Runner* is a flashback to tell Bullet's story–how he attempted to adjust to an overbearing father and how his silent but angry mother, Abigail, tries to cope with her domineering husband. The characterization of the four children offers finely chiseled profiles: responsible Dicey, scholarly James, shy but musically talented Maybeth, and stubborn Sammy. The stories will grip the interest of intermediate grade readers as they get caught up with the problems faced by the insecure children. Noting the changes in the children as they get to know their grandmother and begin to feel secure helps the reader appreciate character change. The mellowing of the embittered grandmother also will be noted by the reader of *Homecoming* and *Dicey's Song,* as Abigail and the children grow into a trusting and caring family.

Character traits may be revealed in a few sentences or paragraphs; character change, however, demands much greater treatment, usually a full length novel. Sometimes the same character appears in a series of books. In this case, the change may occur across books, as illustrated in Cynthia Voigt's books about the Tillermans. Other books that can be used to show character change are *Queenie Peevy* (Burch), *The One in the Middle Is the Green Kangaroo* (Blume), *Good Night, Mr. Tom* (Magorian), and *Soccer Duel* (Dygard).

Recognizing and Appreciating Different Types of Literature

Intermediate grade level guidebooks of most basal reading series suggest giving instruction in recognizing different types or genres of literature. Most types are included in pupil texts starting at the primer or first reader level. These include folk and fairy tales, myths and legends, poetry, realistic fiction, historical fiction, fantasy, biography, and tall tales. Before receiving instruction in recognizing a type of literature, students need ample opportunities to read, hear, or enjoy numerous selections of that literary type. They can identify characteristics of a form if they have a rich background of experience to draw upon.

Folklore. Some children meet folk and fairy tales first in primers or first reader level texts; others will have heard folk and fairy tales told by parents or nursery school or kindergarten teachers. Well-known fairy tales, such as "Little Red Riding Hood" and "Cinderella," have been retold and illustrated beautifully by several contemporary writers and artists. Collect several versions of the same tale for children to enjoy; then compare the retellings

*Illustration from **Little Red Riding Hood** retold by B.G. Ford, illustrated by Elve Fortis De Hieronymis. Text copyright © 1985 by Grosset & Dunlap, Inc., copyright © 1984 La Coccinella Editrice, Varese. Reprinted by permission.*

and illustrations. "Little Red Riding Hood" is frequently included in pupil texts. Trade books telling the same story include Elve Fortis de Hieronymis's *Little Riding Hood,* Trina Schart Hyman's *Little Red Riding Hood,* and Beatrice Schenk de Regniers's *Red Riding Hood,* which is told in verse. Children will grow as critical readers by comparing two or more of these versions with the one included in the pupil text.

Many writers and illustrators have presented their interpretation of well known fairy tales. A few of these are *The Princess and the Pea* (Stevens), *The Snow Queen* (Zeldich), *Cinderella* (Galdone), *Hansel and Gretel* (Lesser), and *The Sleeping Beauty* (Hyman).

An excellent compendium of black folktales collected by Virginia Hamilton is *The People Could Fly: American Black Folktales.* Hamilton retells twenty-four tales, adds appropriate commentary, and lists thirty-six books that include other versions of black folktales.

The major concern in using most books of folk and fairy tales should be to enhance enjoyment in reading. A serendipitious side effect is that students will also develop an

*Illustration from **Little Red Riding Hood** retold and illustrated by Trina Schart Hyman. Copyright © 1983 by Trina Schart Hyman. Holiday House. Reprinted by permission.*

Cover illustration from **Tomie dePaola's Mother Goose.** Copyright © 1985 by Tomie dePaola. G.P. Putnam's Sons. Reprinted by permission.

appreciation for the history and culture of a people. Beginners will benefit from knowing the "classic" folktales, some of which may be told or read to the children by the teacher. Most students can wait until several years later to learn to recognize the characteristics of folk and fairy tales from various countries. Appreciation of the stories is paramount at all levels.

Pupil texts at primary grade levels frequently include several Mother Goose rhymes with appropriate accompanying pictures. After using a Mother Goose rhyme in reading instruction, read other rhymes to the children. Though many illustrated Mother Goose rhyme collections have been published, two recent ones (both beautifully illustrated) are *Tomie dePaola's Mother Goose* and Michael

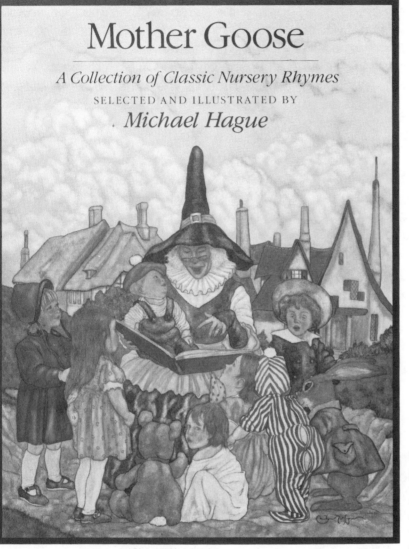

Illustration from **Mother Goose,** selected and illustrated by Michael Hague. Illustrations copyright © 1984 by Michael Hague. Holt, Rinehart and Winston. Reprinted by permission.

Hague's *Mother Goose*. Contrast the illustrations accompanying a rhyme in the basal reader pupil text or in a Mother Goose collection with illustrations of the same rhyme by a different illustrator.

Myths and legends. Still another type of literature included in pupil texts is the myth. Usually such stories offer a simplistic explanation of some aspect of nature or of life and involve superhuman beings. Though students may encounter myths at the primary level, recognition of this type of literature usually is not taught until fifth grade or above.

Since many myths included in pupil texts are those of Native Americans, the books cited here are Indian myths and legends. Paul Goble's *Buffalo Woman, The Great Race, The Girl Who Loved Wild Horses,* and *Star Boy* are all beautifully told and illustrated myths. John Steptoe's *The Story of Jumping Mouse* and Olaf Baker's *Where the Buffaloes Begin* relate Indian legends. These books are good myths and legends for students to read along with the basal text. The attractive illustrations add considerably to the stories depicted, and the myths and legends offer insight into the culture of American Indians of earlier times.

Realistic fiction. Realistic fiction is frequently included in pupil texts. Such selections depict characters and their actions in keeping with real life, and examples are easy to find because this is one of the most frequently encountered literary type in trade books. For further illustration of this literary type, teachers may use books by Beverly Cleary, Betsy Byars, and Cynthia Voigt referred to earlier. A few examples of the many thousands of trade books that may be used to give students further exposure to realistic fiction are cited here. *When I Was Young in the Mountains* (Rylant), relates in words and pictures the story of a girl growing up some years ago in the mountains. *Mustard* (Graeber) tells of a family's reactions to the aging and ultimate death of the family cat. *Like Jake and Me* (Jukes) is the story of a young boy growing in his relationship with his stepfather.

Historical fiction. One last literary type to be mentioned is historical fiction, which frequently is included in pupil texts. The story, which is realistic fiction set in a historical period, sometimes includes actual historical figures, such as Benjamin Franklin or Abraham Lincoln. Sometimes the characters and the story are fictional, but the setting is historically accurate and story events are in line with history. *My Brother Sam Is Dead* (Collier and Collier) and *Across Five Aprils* (Hunt) are good examples of this literary type. The first is set amidst the turmoil of the American Revolution, while the second tells of the divided loyalty of a southern Illinois family in the American Civil War. The Laura Ingalls Wilder books, such as *The Little House in the Big Woods,* are also good examples of this literary genre.

Joan W. Blos's *A Gathering of Days,* a Newbery Medal winner, reveals in diary format what a young girl's life was like growing up in New Hampshire in the early 1830s. Jean Fritz has written a number of humorous books about important characters in early American history, including *What's the Big Idea, Ben Franklin?; And Then What Happened, Paul Revere?;* and *Where Was Patrick Henry on the 29th of May?* These and many other books help teachers bring history and historical characters to life for students. Further, through such books, students can gain a greater understanding of what life was like in earlier times.

In Conclusion

Teachers should capitalize on every opportunity to encourage students to read good children's books. In classrooms in which basal reading series are used as core instructional materials, numerous opportunities occur to motivate students to read more. Some of this extended reading may be done in school; some of it may be done outside of school when children have the time and the desire to read. Much of the extended reading should be in the form of reading aloud by the teacher, with the total class participating as listeners and discussants. Whatever patterns teachers use, they must avoid overanalyzing a selection lest it kill children's interest in reading. Too much teacher supervision of students' independent reading can lead students to view reading as "work" rather than pleasure. Further, if a book is read aloud to students, or they are requested to read it for a skill related purpose (as in the two skills clusters discussed), the teacher must carefully select books that lend themselves to reinforcing this particular skill. Wise teachers will avoid spending so much time on the skill instruction that interest in the content will be destroyed.

Reading teachers are ever mindful of that part of the instructional program that enhances reading skills and, at the same time, moves students toward becoming readers who not only *know how* to read but *will* read, and will continue to be readers through life. Teachers know they must provide time to read and make good books readily available if students are to become lifelong readers.

Children's Books

Baker, Olaf. *Where the Buffaloes Begin.* Illustrated by Stephen Gammell. Warne, 1981.

Blos, Joan W. *A Gathering of Days.* Scribner's, 1979.

Blume, Judy. *The One in the Middle Is the Green Kangaroo.* Illustrated by Amy Aitken. Bradbury, 1981.

Burch, Robert. *Christmas with Ida Early.* Viking, 1983.

Burch, Robert. *Ida Early Comes Over the Mountain.* Viking, 1980.

Burch, Robert. *Queenie Peevy.* Viking, 1976.

Burch, Robert. *Two that Were Tough.* Viking, 1976.

Byars, Betsy. *The Computer Nut.* Viking, 1984.

Byars, Betsy. *Cracker Jackson.* Viking, 1985.

Byars, Betsy. *The Cybil War.* Viking, 1981.

Byars, Betsy. *The Glory Girl.* Viking, 1983.

Byars, Betsy. *The Not-Just-Anybody Family.* Delacorte, 1986.

Byars, Betsy. *The Pinballs.* Harper and Row, 1977.

Byars, Betsy. *The Summer of the Swans.* Viking, 1970.

Cleary, Beverly. *Dear Mr. Henshaw.* Morrow, 1983.

Cleary, Beverly. *Lucky Chuck.* Illustrated by J. Winslow Higginbottom. Morrow, 1984.

Cleary, Beverly. *Ralph S. Mouse.* Morrow, 1982.

Cleary, Beverly. *Ramona Forever.* Morrow, 1984.

Cleary, Beverly. *Ramona Quimby, Age 8.* Morrow, 1981.

Cleary, Beverly. *Ramona and Her Father.* Morrow, 1977.

Cleary, Beverly. *Ramona and Her Mother.* Morrow, 1979.

Collier, James Lincoln, and Collier, Christopher. *My Brother Sam Is Dead.* Four Winds, 1974.

de Hieronymis, Elve Fortis. *Little Red Riding Hood.* Grosset, 1985.

dePaola, Tomie. *Tomie dePaola's Mother Goose.* Putnam's, 1985.

de Regniers, Beatrice Schenk. *Red Riding Hood.* Illustrated by Edward Gorey. Atheneum, 1972.

Dygard, Thomas J. *Soccer Duel.* Morrow, 1981.

Forbes, Esther. *Johnny Tremain.* Houghton Mifflin, 1946.

Fox, Paula. *One-Eyed Cat.* Bradbury, 1984.

Fritz, Jean. *And Then What Happened, Paul Revere?* Illustrated by Margot Tomes. Coward, McCann and Geoghegan, 1976.

Fritz, Jean. *What's the Big Idea, Ben Franklin?* Illustrated by Margot Tomes. Coward, McCann and Geoghegan, 1976.

Fritz, Jean. *Where Was Patrick Henry on the 29th of May?* Illustrated by Margot Tomes. Coward, McCann and Geoghegan, 1975.

Galdone, Paul. *Cinderella.* McGraw-Hill, 1978.

Goble, Paul. *Buffalo Woman.* Bradbury, 1984.

Goble, Paul. *The Girl Who Loved Wild Horses.* Bradbury, 1978.

Goble, Paul. *The Great Race.* Bradbury, 1985.

Goble, Paul. *Star Boy.* Bradbury, 1983.

Graeber, Charlotte. *Mustard.* Illustrated by Donna Diamond. Macmillan, 1982.

Grahame, Kenneth. *The Wind in the Willows.* Dell, 1969.

Hague, Michael. *Mother Goose.* Holt, Rinehart and Winston, 1984.

Hamilton, Virginia. *The People Could Fly: American Black Folktales.* Illustrated by Leo and Diane Dillon. Knopf, 1985.

Hunt, Irene. *Across Five Aprils.* Grosset and Dunlap, 1964.

Hyman, Trina Schart. *Little Red Riding Hood.* Holiday, 1983.

Hyman, Trina Schart. *The Sleeping Beauty.* Little, Brown, 1977.

Jukes, Mavis. *Like Jake and Me.* Illustrated by Lloyd Bloom. Knopf, 1984.

Lesser, Rika. *Hansel and Gretel.* Illustrated by Paul O. Zelinsky. Dodd, Mead, 1984.

Livingston, Myra Cohn. *Sea Songs.* Illustrated by Leonard Everett Fisher. Holiday, 1986.

Livingston, Myra Cohn. *A Song I Sing to You.* Illustrated by Margot Tomes. Harcourt Brace Jovanovich, 1984.

Magorian, Michelle. *Good Night, Mr. Tom.* Harper and Row, 1981.

Milne, A.A. *Winnie the Pooh.* Dutton, 1926.

Prelutsky, Jack. *It's Snowing! It's Snowing!* Illustrated by Jeanne Titherington. Greenwillow, 1984.

Prelutsky, Jack. *My Parents Think I'm Sleeping.* Illustrated by Yossi Abolafia. Greenwillow, 1985.

Prelutsky, Jack. *The Random House Book of Poetry for Children.* Illustrated by Arnold Lobel. Random House, 1983.

Rylant, Cynthia. *When I Was Young in the Mountains.* Illustrated by Dianne Goode. Dutton, 1982.

Silverstein, Shel. *A Light in the Attic.* Harper and Row, 1981.

Silverstein, Shel. *Where the Sidewalk Ends.* Harper and Row, 1974.

Steptoe, John. *The Story of Jumping Mouse.* Lothrop, 1984.

Stevens, Janet. *The Princess and the Pea.* Holiday, 1982.

Voigt, Cynthia. *Dicey's Song.* Atheneum, 1982.

Voigt, Cynthia. *Homecoming.* Atheneum, 1981.

Voigt, Cynthia. *The Runner.* Atheneum, 1985.

White, E.B. *Charlotte's Web.* Illustrated by Garth Williams. Harper and Row, 1952.

Wilder, Laura Ingalls. *Little House in the Big Woods.* Harper and Row, 1932.

Zeldich, Arieh. *The Snow Queen.* Harper and Row, 1985.

Chapter 12

The Republic of Childhood and the Reading Disabled

Roselmina Indrisano
Jeanne R. Paratore

Yes, children's books keep alive a sense of nationality; but they also keep alive a sense of humanity. They describe their native land lovingly, but they also describe faraway lands where unknown brothers live. They understand the essential quality of their own race; but each of them is a messenger that goes beyond mountains and rivers, beyond the seas, to the very ends of the world in search of new friendships. Every country gives and every country receives–innumerable are the exchanges–and so it comes about that in our first impressionable years the universal republic of childhood is born (Hazard, 1944, p. 146).

These elegant words offer insights into the extraordinary value of literature for children. During the years we have worked with reading disabled learners, we have noted that many of these children have not become citizens of the "republic of childhood." Professionals who are responsible for these children's learning often focus exclusively on skills instruction to the neglect of the world of children's literature. Bearing in mind the need for both instruction and enjoyment, we offer approaches to using children's literature to develop competent and caring readers. The strategies may be used with literary selections in reading texts and with recommended trade books. The ideas have been used effectively with children who are reading disabled.

Background

In this chapter, we focus on two areas of learning that help improve reading abilities and foster competent readers: concept literacy and pattern literacy. Concept literacy results not only from owning words and their meanings, but also from owning schemata that reflect the relationship of the concepts to one another and to the world. Approaches to developing concept literacy are designed to assist reading disabled learners to own the schemata and to relate them to the schemata of the writer. The efficacy of this approach, going beyond mere word recognition to word relationships, is affirmed by Brown and Campione (1985, p. 19):

Remedial reading procedures have a heavy skills mastery emphasis; and the skills to be mastered tend to be primarily "word attack" practice. Comprehension instruction is rare. Simply stated, the current state of affairs is that poor readers, particularly those labeled as mildly retarded, are unlikely in the present system to develop adequate reading comprehension skills...practice makes possible; if so, perhaps we should not be surprised to find a cumulative deficit in comprehension skills in those who do not receive systematic and sustained experience in comprehension fostering activities.

Pattern literacy relates to the structure of the text. The organizational pattern of a text offers a map of the writer's mind. The approaches we suggest emphasize that the organizational pattern of the text relates to the author's purpose and to the content of the selection and that there are a variety of ways authors organize the content. Our primary emphasis here is on expository text.

In a recent study, intermediate grade "poor readers" were taught story mapping procedures with promising results (Idol-Maestas & Croll, 1985).

In discussing the implications of their study, the researchers suggest (p. 26):

> The findings of this study support the position of schema theorists...that when the readers possess or are provided with relevant schemata, a relationship can be drawn between those schemata and the reading materials. In this case, an attempt was made to assist poor comprehenders in building a set of generic, structural schemata (the story map components) that could be applied to narrative stories. The result was that all readers improved their comprehension, and maintenance effects were demonstrated for the majority of them.

Concept Literacy

Language awareness and language use are both part of the development of concept literacy. In the following section, we will describe each of these aspects and suggest appropriate children's books and instructional strategies for developing them.

Language Awareness

Many students who have difficulty with reading have had limited experiences with print. Others have been surrounded by books in their environment, but find the reading process too labored to be willing to read frequently. As a result, they are unfamiliar with the syntactic and semantic variations commonly found in written language, but seldom heard in oral conversation. Strategies for building language and language awareness should focus on the vocabulary and syntax frequently used by writers. A related goal is to build familiarity with a variety of writing styles and a conscious awareness of the author's purpose in selecting the language used to convey the message.

Peggy Parish's *Amelia Bedelia* and its sequels provide excellent opportunities for building awareness of the multiple meanings of words, for discussing the author's use of language, and for calling attention to the literal meanings the author uses to create humor. Other books appropriate for these purposes include *Morris Goes to School* (Wiseman), *I Met a Man* (Ciardi), *The King Who Rained* and *A Chocolate Moose for Dinner* (Gwynne), *Harold and the Purple Crayon* (Johnson), *Animals Should Definitely Not Wear Clothing* and *Animals Should Definitely Not Act Like People* (Barrett), and *The Phantom Tollbooth* (Juster).

Books that help to extend children's awareness of varied syntactic and semantic patterns and assist them in understanding the language of literature include *Amos and Boris* and *Abel's Island* (Steig), *When The Sky Is Like*

Indrisano and Paratore

Lace (Horowitz), *The Wind in the Willows* (Grahame), and *Annie and the Old One* (Miles).

To help reading disabled students develop language awareness, begin by reading and enjoying the book with the children. The discussion that follows focuses on the intended learning. For example, having read and laughed over *Amelia Bedelia,* the discussion can center on Peggy Parish's use of words that cause the reader to enjoy the humor of the situations. In *Merry Christmas, Amelia Be-* *delia,* Amelia "trims the tree"–with a pair of hedge trimming shears.

Language Production

Children's literature helps to clarify concepts and shows that language represents meanings. When a child reads about a hawk in *Hawk, I'm Your Brother* (Baylor), the combination of text and illustration contribute to an understanding of the creature and its characteristics. We have found that this understanding facilitates oral and written language

Teaching Idea

Clarifying Concepts

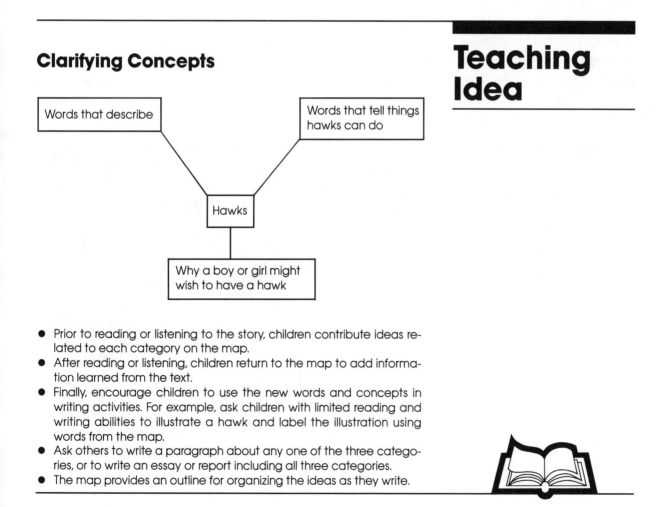

- Prior to reading or listening to the story, children contribute ideas related to each category on the map.
- After reading or listening, children return to the map to add information learned from the text.
- Finally, encourage children to use the new words and concepts in writing activities. For example, ask children with limited reading and writing abilities to illustrate a hawk and label the illustration using words from the map.
- Ask others to write a paragraph about any one of the three categories, or to write an essay or report including all three categories.
- The map provides an outline for organizing the ideas as they write.

production. Semantic mapping strategies developed by Johnson and Pearson (1985) are particularly useful for helping readers and writers organize and interrelate essential ideas and supporting details. Having read *Hawk, I'm Your Brother*, students can map the characteristics of the bird and keep them for comparison to the next creature they study.

Another use of the semantic map in clarifying concepts and in facilitating language production is as a prereading or prelistening discussion guide. For reading disabled learners, the visual display shows the words and the relationships among the ideas they represent. The semantic map visually displays the words and the relationships among the ideas the words represent. Such a map facilitates students' abilities to classify and organize ideas.

Books related to science and social studies that are particularly helpful in developing concept literacy include *Freight Train* (Crews),

What's Hatching Out of that Egg? (Lauber), *If You Are a Hunter of Fossils* (Baylor), and *Birth of an Island* (Selsam).

Pattern Literacy

Recent research suggests that well-written expository prose conforms to an identifiable pattern or writing plan, characterized as cause/effect, comparison/contrast, time order, response (problem/solution), or description (Meyer, 1984). Investigations reveal that students who have an explicit awareness of text patterns improve comprehension (Meyer & Rice, 1984; Taylor, 1982; Taylor & Beach, 1984). Yet children experiencing difficulty in reading often fail to use the text's organizational pattern to assist them in recalling and understanding what they read. They are unable to organize information they read. Recall protocols of reading disabled learners (Paratore, 1983) reveal a focus on unimportant and irrel-

*From **Ox-Cart Man** by Donald Hall. Pictures by Barbara Cooney. Illustrations copyright © 1979 by Barbara Cooney Porter. Reprinted by permission of Viking Penguin, Inc.*

Indrisano and Paratore

Comparison

- Summary: *Two Islands* (Gantschev) is the story of two places that were similar until people settled there. Because of the attitudes of the two groups of settlers, the islands become very different.
- Objectives: Throughout this book, the organizational pattern is comparison/contrast. To help students comprehend and retain these ideas, an idea map provides an advance organizer.
- Plan: The setting for the story is recorded in the map shown. Ask students to read to find out how the two islands are alike and how they are different.

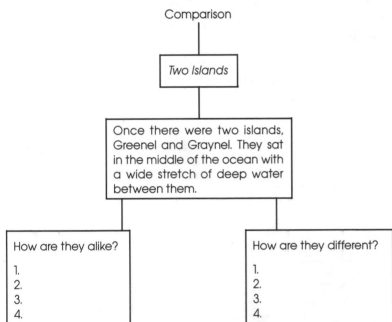

Comparison

Two Islands

Once there were two islands, Greenel and Graynel. They sat in the middle of the ocean with a wide stretch of deep water between them.

How are they alike?
1.
2.
3.
4.

How are they different?
1.
2.
3.
4.

*Illustration from **Two Islands** by Ivan Gantschev. Copyright © 1985. Published in USA by Picture Book Studio USA, an imprint of Neugebauer Press USA Inc. Reprinted by permission.*

- After reading, students use the map to assist them in recalling and understanding the author's ideas and for recording important details.
- Initial discussion focuses on the text pattern, helping students to develop a strategy for organizing and recalling information read.
- Encourage students to consider both explicit and implicit details. For example, in this selection, discussion of the characters' motives and goals are important to understanding the development of each island. Though not explicitly stated, this information can be inferred and can be effectively discussed within the comparison/contrast framework.
- After completing the discussion, ask students to use their pattern maps to write about the selection, facilitating retention of story ideas and concepts and also providing practice in the use of a particular pattern in their own writing.

evant information and an inability to organize recall in a cohesive manner. The brief text and vivid illustrations of picture books make these excellent resources for the development of pattern literacy for children who are reading disabled.

Comparison

A method for teaching comparison is described in the accompanying teaching idea. Additional titles for developing awareness of comparison/contrast as a text pattern include *Town and Country* (Provensen & Provensen), *The Little House* (Burton), *A Special Trade* (Wittman), *The Bear's Bicycle* (McLeod), and *Amos and Boris* (Steig).

Sequence

A similar instructional approach is used for introducing students to sequential patterns. (See Figure 1.) Using *Ox-Cart Man* (Hall), ask students to provide supporting details for each event specified. Help students focus on essential information first, recalling all main events, and then ask them to supply supporting details for major events. For example: Was the ox cart man reluctant to sell his ox? What in the text and illustration makes you think so? How does the economic cycle of the family shown in this historical period differ from ours today?

Additional titles for developing an awareness of sequence of time order as a prose pattern include *Charlie Needs a Cloak* (de-

Figure 1

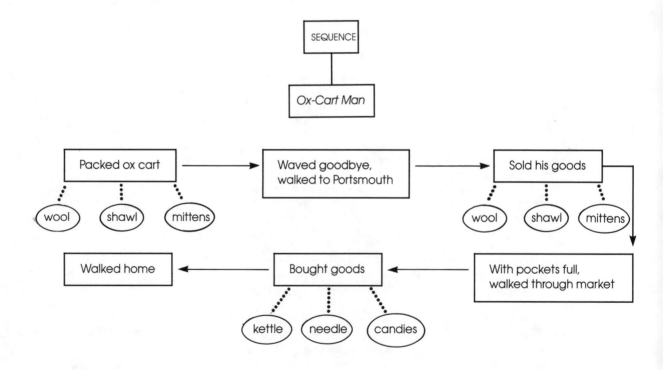

Indrisano and Paratore

Paola), *How Puppies Grow* and *How Kittens Grow* (Selsam), *The Very Hungry Caterpillar* (Carle), and *And Then What Happened, Paul Revere?* (Fritz).

Description

Description is a pattern that expands knowledge of a specific concept. *Harbor* (Crews) contributes to readers' understanding and ability to define and describe a concept; in this instance, harbors. Use the book as a resource for creating the type of map in Figure 2 based on description.

Additional titles appropriate for developing awareness of description or listing as a prose pattern include *Anno's Journey* (Anno),

The Little Island (MacDonald), *The Big Snow* (Hader and Hader), and *Truck* (Crews).

Causation

Since understanding causation requires awareness of sequence in which events occurred, students are reminded of the importance of the order of events when recalling cause and effect relationships. Plot the events of the story to show how one event becomes the cause of another. Chaining the cause and effect makes them visible and, therefore, memorable. (See Figure 3.)

Additional titles for developing an awareness of causation as a prose pattern include *Why Mosquitoes Buzz in People's Ears* (Aar-

Figure 2

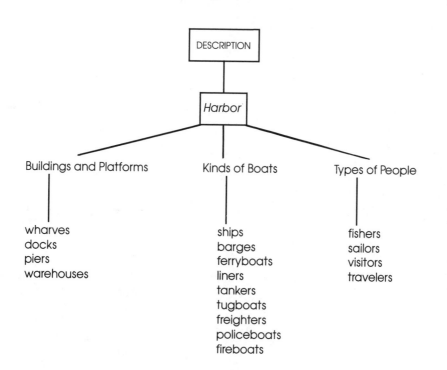

Figure 3

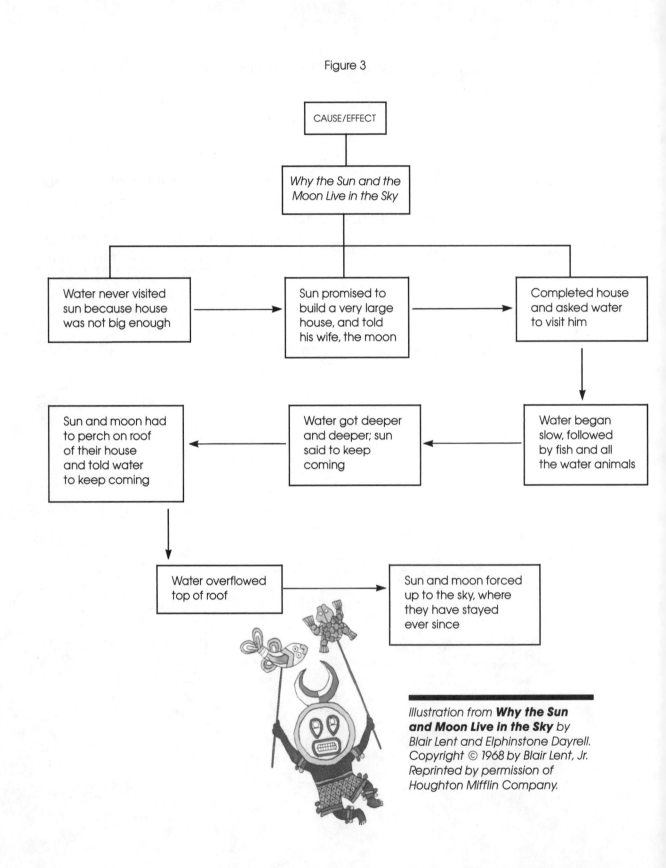

```
                        ┌──────────────────┐
                        │   CAUSE/EFFECT   │
                        └────────┬─────────┘
                                 │
                    ┌────────────┴───────────┐
                    │  Why the Sun and the   │
                    │  Moon Live in the Sky  │
                    └────────────┬───────────┘
```

Water never visited sun because house was not big enough → Sun promised to build a very large house, and told his wife, the moon → Completed house and asked water to visit him

↓

Sun and moon had to perch on roof of their house and told water to keep coming ← Water got deeper and deeper; sun said to keep coming ← Water began slow, followed by fish and all the water animals

↓

Water overflowed top of roof → Sun and moon forced up to the sky, where they have stayed ever since

*Illustration from **Why the Sun and Moon Live in the Sky** by Blair Lent and Elphinstone Dayrell. Copyright © 1968 by Blair Lent, Jr. Reprinted by permission of Houghton Mifflin Company.*

Indrisano and Paratore

*Illustration from **Harbor** by Donald Crews. Copyright © 1982 by Donald Crews. Greenwillow Books, a division of William Morrow and Company, Inc. Reprinted by permission.*

dema), *The Adventures of Spider* (Arkhurst), *Foolish Rabbit's Big Mistake* (Martin), and *It Could Always Be Worse* (Zemach).

Conclusion

In this chapter, we have presented approaches to the development of concept literacy and pattern literacy with an emphasis on reading disabled children. A final word is in order. Time and space limit our capacity to extend our discussion to the effect of reading fine classic and modern literature. In our view, being introduced to these works in ways that make the reading a satisfying experience is, for the reading disabled learner, the beginning of the capacity for aesthetic response. The first step to citizenship in the "republic of childhood" is the ability and the opportunity to engage in conversation with those who are its most noble observers. Such conversation is the right of every learner and the responsibility of every teacher.

References

Brown, Ann L., and Campione, Joseph C. *Psychological theory and the study of learning disabilities.* Technical Report No. 360. Urbana, IL: Center for the Study of Reading, 1985.

Hazard, Paul. *Books, children and men.* Boston: The Horn Book, 1944.

Idol-Maestas, Lorna, and Croll, Valerie J. *The effects of training in story mapping procedures on the reading comprehension of poor readers.* Technical Report No. 352. Urbana, IL: Center for the Study of Reading, 1985.

Johnson, Dale D., and Pearson, P. David. *Teaching reading vocabulary.* New York: Holt, Rinehart and Winston, 1985.

Meyer, Bonnie J.F. Organizational aspects of texts: Effects on reading comprehension and application for the classroom. In James Flood (Ed.), *Promoting reading comprehension.* Newark, DE: International Reading Association, 1984.

Meyer, Bonnie J.F., and Rice, Elizabeth. The structure of text. In P. David Pearson (Ed.), *Handbook of reading research.* New York: Longman, 1984.

Paratore, Jeanne R. The influence of reader interest and reader prior knowledge on the reading performance of fourth grade unskilled readers, within the context of a clinical assessment. Unpublished doctoral dissertation, Boston University, 1983.

Taylor, Barbara. Text structure and children's comprehension and memory for expository material. *Journal of Educational Psychology,* 1982, *74,* 323-340.

Taylor, Barbara, and Beach, Richard. The effects of text structure instruction on middle-grade students' comprehension and production of expository text. *Reading Research Quarterly,* 1984, *19,* 134-146.

Children's Books

Aardema, Verna. *Why Mosquitoes Buzz in People's Ears.* Illustrated by Leo Dillon and Diane Dillon. Dial, 1975.

Anno, Mitsumasa. *Anno's Journey.* Philomel, 1977.

Arkhurst, Joyce Cooper. *The Adventures of Little Spider.* Illustrated by Jerry Pinkney. Little, Brown, 1964.

Barrett, Judi. *Animals Should Definitely Not Act Like People.* Illustrated by Ron Barrett. Atheneum, 1980.

Barrett, Judi. *Animals Should Definitely Not Wear Clothing.* Atheneum, 1970.

Baylor, Byrd. *Hawk, I'm Your Brother.* Illustrated by Peter Parnall. Charles Scribner's Sons, 1976.

Baylor, Byrd. *If You Are a Hunter of Fossils.* Illustrated by Peter Parnall. Atheneum, 1980.

Burton, Virginia Lee. *The Little House.* Houghton Mifflin, 1942.

Carle, Eric. *The Very Hungry Caterpillar.* Philomel, 1969.

Ciardi, John. *I Met a Man.* Boston: Houghton Mifflin, 1961.

Crews, Donald. *Freight Train.* Greenwillow, 1978.

Crews, Donald. *Harbor.* Greenwillow, 1982.

Crews, Donald. *Truck.* Greenwillow, 1980.

Dayrell, Elphinstone. *Why the Sun and the Moon Live in the Sky.* Illustrated by Blair Lent. Houghton Mifflin, 1968.

dePaola, Tomie. *Charlie Needs a Cloak.* Prentice Hall, 1974.

Fritz, Jean. *And Then What Happened, Paul Revere?* Illustrated by Margot Tomes. Coward, 1973.

Gantschev, Ivan. *Two Islands.* Picture Book Studio, 1985.

Grahame, Kenneth. *The Wind in the Willows.* Illustrated by Ernest H. Shepard. Scribner, 1933.

Gwynne, Fred. *A Chocolate Moose for Dinner.* Messner, 1970.

Gwynne, Fred. *The King Who Rained.* Messner, 1970.

Hader, Berta, and Elmer Hader. *The Big Snow.* Macmillan, 1948.

Hall, Donald. *Ox-Cart Man.* Illustrated by Barbara Cooney. Viking, 1979.

Horowitz, Elinor L. *When the Sky Is Like Lace.* Illustrated by Barbara Cooney. Lippincott, 1975.

Johnson, Crockett. *Harold and the Purple Crayon.* Harper and Row, 1955.

Juster, Norton. *The Phantom Tollbooth.* Random House, 1961.

Lauber, Patricia. *What's Hatching Out of that Egg?* Crown, 1979.

MacDonald, Golden. *The Little Island.* Illustrated by Leonard Weisgard. Doubleday, 1946.

Martin, Rafe. *Foolish Rabbit's Big Mistake.* Illustrated by Ed Young. G.P. Putnam's Sons, 1985.

McLeod, Emilie W. *The Bear's Bicycle.* Illustrated by David McPhail. Atlantic-Little, Brown, 1975.

Miles, Miska. *Annie and the Old One.* Illustrated by Peter Parnall. Little, Brown, 1971.

Parish, Peggy. *Amelia Bedelia.* Illustrated by Fritz Siebel. Harper and Row, 1963.

Parish, Peggy. *Merry Christmas, Amelia Bedelia.* Illustrated by Lynn Sweat. Greenwillow, 1986.

Provensen, Alice, and Martin Provensen. *Town and Country.* Crown, 1984.

Selsam, Millicent E. *Birth of an Island.* Illustrated by Winifred Lubell. Harper and Row, 1959.

Selsam, Millicent E. *How Kittens Grow.* Illustrated by Esther Bubley. Four Winds, 1975.

Selsam, Milicent E. *How Puppies Grow.* Illustrated by Esther Bubley. Four Winds, 1972.

Steig, William. *Abel's Island.* Farrar, Straus and Giroux, 1976.

Steig, William. *Amos and Boris.* Farrar, Straus and Giroux, 1971.

Wiseman, B. *Morris Goes to School.* Harper, 1970.

Wittman, Sally. *A Special Trade.* Illustrated by Karen Gundersheimer. Harper and Row, 1978.

Zemach, Margot. *It Could Always Be Worse.* Farrar, Straus and Giroux, 1977.

Chapter 13
California Reading Initiative

Francie Alexander

INTRODUCTION TO CALIFORNIA READING INITIATIVE*

Bernice E. Cullinan

On May 9, 1986, Bill Honig, State Superintendent of Public Instruction in California, launched the California Reading Initiative. About the initiative, which serves as a model of how literature can be integrated into a reading program, he said,

> Reading is one of the most effective ways of learning. I want to encourage students to read and I want them to enjoy reading. Good reading skills are critical to success in *all* academic areas. We are launching the California Reading Initiative to address serious concerns about students' reading abilities and practices. Recent figures indicate that we are experiencing an alarming increase in illiteracy in this nation. Many of our students who can read are having difficulty understanding what they read. Further, many of our students who can read and who can understand what they read simply don't read.
>
> The California Reading Initiative has been developed to address these concerns. An important part of our strategy is to improve reading instruction and to provide students access to good books. A love of reading and books is one of the most important gifts that teachers and parents can give our young people.

Honig described the comprehensive plan developed to undergird and accomplish these goals. In July 1985, he appointed a committee to develop a list of books to be recommended to the three million kindergarten through eighth grade students in California. The list was to be a companion document to the list issued earlier for ninth to twelfth grade students. Teachers, librarians, administrators, and members of the superintendent's ethnic advisory panels served on the committee, which was asked to identify books that could convey our literary heritage to young

The California Reading Initiative committee produced a list of 1,010 books divided into three sections: core, extended, and recreational. The lists are divided into two parts, one for K-six and one for seventh and eighth grades. The core literature includes selections to be taught in the

---

*Note: Introduction based on the Books in the Classroom column, *The Horn Book*, November/December 1986.

classroom—selections to be read closely for consideration as a stimulus for writing and discussion. Books from the extended literature list will be assigned to individual students or small groups to supplement class work. The recreational and motivational literature will be recommended by teachers and librarians for students' leisure reading. The seventh and eighth grade books are intended to appeal to the broadening tastes of that age group.

Associate Superintendent Francie Alexander points out that the list is "a living list" that will grow and change; it is not carved in bronze. Alexander also emphasizes that a list of books alone cannot do the job needed to affect how reading is taught to children. One of four major strategies underway to insure success of the program involves curriculum development. Teachers and librarians are working on the *English-Language Arts Framework,* described in detail in Alexander's article. The framework addresses independent reading, a literature based curriculum, and literary works as models and as stimulus for writing and developing other language related skills. In addition to the framework, the *English-Language Arts Model Curriculum Guide* contains a compendium of activities to show how to teach reading using trade books and other materials in the classroom. These activities, supported by the *Handbook for Planning an Effective Literature Program* that describes how high quality literature can be used to shape curriculum, are tied to books on the kindergarten through eighth grade list. There are examples of how to use many of the books.

Honig and Alexander know, however, that a list of books, an *English-Language Arts Framework,* a model curriculum guide, and a literature handbook will not assure the kind of results they want. They know the teacher is the key to what happens in any classroom; therefore, they have a comprehensive plan for staff development seminars and workshops to be conducted across California to help teachers implement this program.

Another major strategy Honig and Alexander are putting into action is test development. They have heard too many teachers say, "I know students should read good books. I know I should read aloud to them. I know they should have time to read on their own, but their progress is measured by standardized tests, and there is no payoff on the tests." Honig and Alexander are trying to change the testing program so that it does not distort instruction. One immediate step is to have eighth grade students complete a writing test as well as the typical multiple choice test. They feel assured students with a broad background in reading will do well on the writing test; some of the questions require youngsters to write about things they have read.

When schools change the nature of the materials used in instructional programs, they need the help of publishers. The resource development program depends upon the cooperation of publishers, school and public librarians, classroom teachers, administrators, supervisors, booksellers, and parents. Further, success depends upon equity through foundation grants and sponsors so that *all* children can have access to good books.

I enjoyed a surge of confidence when I heard Bill Honig's response to the question, "How many of these 1,000 books have you read?" He answered, "About 75 percent of them. And *The Wind in the Willows* is one of my favorites."

The California Reading Initiative was launched by State Superintendent Bill Honig in order to address growing illiteracy, semiliteracy, and aliteracy. The problem of illiteracy has been well documented by recent census data indicating that 13 percent of our citizens are illiterate. There is evidence that semiliteracy should also be of concern. We describe the semiliterate as one who can read but who does not understand what has been read. And finally, aliteracy, which describes the person who can read but chooses not to read, seems particularly wasteful. Perhaps the aliterate experienced learning to read but never recognized the value of reading to learn.

We have been engaged in an educational reform effort that has resulted in a renewed sense of purpose for our schools. We are committed to connecting our students to their political, ethical, and social worlds and know that this can be accomplished only by providing a rich curriculum in science, history, literature, the arts, and other key subjects. The California Reading Initiative recognizes the importance of reading in this endeavor.

The initiative started when Honig released a list of 1,010 good books for students in kindergarten through eighth grade, a companion document to an earlier list for ninth to twelfth graders. The list was a mechanism for articulating the basic themes of the initiative.

• Reading is attainable and pleasurable.

• The emphasis is on readers (students) not readers (books).

• Learning to read is a means toward the goal of becoming a lifelong reader.

• Teachers model and inspire as well as teach.

• Parents are teachers, also. When they read aloud, listen to children read, and encourage reading, they enhance the learning process.

• Literature should be the core of the language arts curriculum.

• Books are treasures that should be accessible to all.

The booklist is part of a comprehensive plan that includes curriculum development, staff development, test development, and resource development. These developmental efforts are the essential elements of the California Reading Initiative.

A look at how reading is taught greatly influenced the developmental efforts now underway. Current methods might be characterized as an assemblyline approach, for we have broken down the reading process into a seemingly endless list of subskills. Students spend significant periods of time analyzing digraphs, coloring pictures that start with the letter (b), and matching pairs of words. However, they spend very little time reading. And when they do read, it is for a purpose that becomes routine. Many students know that if it is Monday, they will be looking for the main idea. It should come as no surprise that students who have mastered the skill and drill curriculum are more experienced at coloring and matching than at reading with comprehension.

So what do youngsters do during the reading period? They complete worksheets. According to *Becoming a Nation of Readers* (Anderson et al., 1985), students spend up to 70 percent of the time allocated for reading instruction on worksheet type activities that "require only a perfunctory level of reading." This situation has prompted writers of the *English-Language Arts Framework for California Public Schools, K-12* to call worksheets "the dismal paperchase of childhood."

The *English-Language Arts Framework* is the foundation document for all state and local curriculum development activities; it is one of four new documents introduced during the 1986-1987 school year, the year called "The Year of the Reader." The Framework sets forth an agenda for changing the curriculum and expands upon the themes of the California Reading Initiative.

• The Framework calls for a literature based program that exposes all students (including those whose primary language is not English) to significant works and encourages reading, rather than a skill based program that uses brief, unfocused narratives and worksheets lacking meaningful content and constructed to teach independent skills in isolation.

• It calls for attention to values through literature reflecting honest dilemmas met by all human beings–often formulated in traditional and modern classics and in good writing from all disciplines, rather than condescending themes catering to superficial values reflected in "safe," sterile texts.

• It calls for a systematic K-12 developmental language arts curriculum that is articulated and implemented at all grade levels, rather than a fragmented curriculum, having little continuity from grade to grade or school to school.

• It calls for instructional programs emphasizing the interaction of listening, speaking, reading, and writing, rather than instructional programs that focus on only one of the language arts at a time, such as reading without purposeful listening, discussion, or writing.

• The Framework calls for a phonics program taught in meaningful contexts, kept simple, and completed in the early grades, rather than an intensive phonics program extending into the middle and upper grades.

• It calls for instructional programs that guide all students through a range of thinking processes as they study content and focus on aesthetic, ethical, and cultural issues, rather than instructional programs that limit some students (e.g., less prepared and limited English proficient) to completing work sheets and activities that address only low level cognitive skills and minimal content.

• The Framework calls for a writing program that includes attention to the various stages of the writing process such as composing, revising, and editing, and teachers who attend to substance first, then form, then correctness, rather than a writing program in which students are merely assigned low level writing, which is read for correctness.

• It calls for subject area teachers who ensure that students read widely, write frequently, and use language effectively, rather than subject area teachers who give to reading and English teachers the whole responsibility of guiding students in acquiring effective language arts and skills.

• It calls for teacher preparation programs that provide candidates with a broad literacy background, an understanding of how to teach higher order thinking skills in meaningful contexts, knowledge of new insights into how children learn, knowledge of where to go for aid as they begin careers and as they design and implement integrated language arts instruction, rather than teacher training programs that emphasize only instructional methodology and the teaching of isolated language skills.

• Finally, the Framework calls for inservice training in advanced knowledge of literature and its approaches, research into working with the limited English proficient (LEP) and students with special needs, rather than inservice programs ignoring recent research and the classroom wisdom teachers can share with one another.

Other documents disseminated during Spring 1987 include *English-Language Arts Model Curriculum Guide* that provides detailed examples and activities for K-8, the *Handbook for Planing an Effective Literature Program* that describes how high quality literary works can be used to shape the K-12 curriculum, and *Recommended Reading in Literature, K-8* that includes recommendations of core, extended, and recreational titles. School districts will use these documents to examine their programs and to design appropriate staff development activities for teachers and administrators.

The California Literature Project exemplifies the kind of high quality staff development programs we are working to implement. The basic premise of the project is that staff development programs require more than two hours or even two days. The project provides a five week summer institute in a university setting.

For those teachers who fear that their students will fail if they do not follow every step in commercially prepared materials, there is a renewed sense of self-confidence about departing from the scripts in the teachers' editions. An unpleasant side effect of the overuse of teachers' manuals is what some have called the "well-managed teacher." Teachers who have participated in the project know how to use literature in the classrooms so that students are engaged and fascinated the way Mole is in *The Wind in the Willows* (Grahame).

Not only do the ubiquitous textbooks and worksheets drive curriculum and instruction, but tests significantly affect what is taught. Fill

Illustration by Ernest H. Shepard from ***The Wind in the Willows.*** *Copyright © 1933 Charles Scribner's Sons; copyright renewed © 1961 Ernest H. Shepard. Reprinted with the permission of Charles Scribner's Sons.*

From **Miss Rumphius** by Barbara Cooney. Copyright © 1982 by Barbara Cooney Porter. Reprinted by permission of Viking Penguin, Inc.

in the blanks and some multiple choice type tests support the fragmentation of the curriculum and reinforce skill and drill activities.

We have tried to meet the challenge of tests that distort the curriculum by adding a direct writing assessment component to the California Assessment Program. In 1987, eighth graders will complete an essay as part of the language test.

The final element, resource development, represents our attempt to connect students to good books. We want them to meet *Caddie Woodlawn* (Brink); Charlotte (*Charlotte's Web*, White); Max (*Where the Wild Things Are*, Sendak); Mike Mulligan (*Mike Mulligan and His Steam Shovel*, Burton); and Alexander (*Alexander and the Terrible, Horrible, No Good, Very Bad Day*, Viorst). We want them to confront important issues and to be exposed to truth, justice, and magnanimity. We

hope to balance a bland diet of materials used to teach reading with books that nourish the mind and heart.

The booklist is the hallmark of this effort; we are working to see that the listed materials are available. Bookstores in California are asked to feature high quality children's literature. Some will display a banner, prepared by Harper & Row Publishers, that proclaims "We support the California Reading Initiative."

The California Reading Initiative has been enthusiastically endorsed by parents, teachers, librarians, school administrators, booksellers, and Mrs. Smith's third grade class. Fran Smith, a mentor teacher at Wildwood Elementary School in Southern California, headed a "Reading Is for Everyone" campaign. As part of the campaign, the local newspaper editor, city planner, and associate superintendent for the State Department of

Education were invited to read their favorite books to the class. These third graders are excited about the prospect of reading all of the books on the list.

One of my favorite books and one that many students will be reading as part of the Young Readers Medal program sponsored by the California Reading Association, is *Miss Rumphius* (Cooney). Miss Rumphius accomplishes her lifetime goal of making the world more beautiful by scattering seeds from which lupine will bloom. Those of us involved in the California Reading Initiative believe that the seeds we scatter will help our students to blossom academically, be engaged in books, be well acquainted with their literary heritage, and possess the literacy necessary to be effective citizens.

Reference

Anderson, Richard C., Heibert, Elfreida H., Scott, Judith A., and Wilkinson, Ian A.G. *Becoming a nation of readers: The report of the Commission on Reading.* Washington: National Institute of Education, 1985.

Children's Books

Brink, Carol R. *Caddie Woodlawn.* Macmillan, 1970.
Burton, Virginia L. *Mike Mulligan and His Steam Shovel.* Houghton Mifflin, 1977.
Cooney, Barbara. *Miss Rumphius.* Viking Penguin, 1982.
Grahame, Kenneth. *The Wind in the Willows.* Illustrated by Ernest H. Shepard. Charles Scribner's Sons, 1961.
Sendak, Maurice. *Where the Wild Things Are.* Harper and Row, 1963.
Viorst, Judith. *Alexander and the Terrible, Horrible, No Good, Very Bad Day.* Atheneum, 1972.
White. E.B. *Charlotte's Web.* Harper & Row, 1952.

Chapter 14
Resources to Identify Children's Books for the Reading Program

Arlene M. Pillar

As a consultant to school districts developing programs for integrating children's literature into the reading curriculum, I have met some outstanding administrators and classroom teachers. Three of them come to mind.

Beverly Lieb teaches second grade and uses "real" books in many creative ways. She is always alert for new and exciting stories to read aloud to her children or to recommend for their private reading; she finds many of the books she uses by browsing the shelves of both the public and the school library; she listens to the children's recommendations, and reads aloud books they have brought to class; she attends professional conferences to learn about recent publications (occasionally she asks me for suggestions); she has begun to build a library of her own. If, for example,

Beverly knows that her students will be reading a story in their basal reader about someone who has acted silly, she will bring two picture books to class: Kathryn Hewitt's *The Three Sillies* and Anne Rockwell's *The Three Sillies and 10 Other Stories to Read Aloud*. Sometimes, Beverly will build a language experience activity from this complementary literature lesson. After discussing ways in which her children have been silly and listing these on a flip chart, she encourages them to write stories of their own. As a result, Beverly Lieb's second grade class learns to read by reading both their basal reader and the "real" books she has made a deliberate effort to find for them. They also learn to read by writing.

Naomi Zimmerman is a reading specialist who teaches fifth and sixth grade reading disabled students. Naomi depends solely on what she calls "fine literature" to educate the youngsters in her charge. She is committed to showing them that reading is meant for the wonderful realistic and fantastic tales woven throughout the ages. She is dedicated to her craft; she reads *all* of the books she recommends to her students. One reason Naomi does this is to avoid the risk of "turning kids off" by recommending inappropriate books. "It takes a great deal of time," she says, "but how can I possibly tell a student to read a wonderful book if I haven't read it? I can only make my enthusiasm contagious when it is genuine. It can only be genuine if I have read the specific book discussed. I truly love reading children's books, and I don't see this as a job; I see it as a joy." Naomi finds the books she reads in the same places Lieb does. She also takes university courses in children's literature. I know that when her students begin to study the United States' expansion, she will read aloud Jean Fritz's *Make Way for Sam Houston,* on my recommendation.

Carol Silver is a middle school librarian. She is the expert for the students in her school and for many of her colleagues. Where does *she*

*Illustration by Elise Primavera reprinted by permission of G.P. Putnam's Sons from **Make Way for Sam Houston** by Jean Fritz, illustrations copyright © 1986 by Elise Primavera.*

Resources to Identify Children's Books

find the books she tells them about? Her resources are many. For example, if a sixth grade teacher asks for a read aloud book that is not too long and that will capture the imagination with vivid imagery, Carol knows from broad reading that Paul Fleischman's *Coming-and-Going Men* is just what that teacher needs. Carol's expertise has been built with years of patient commitment to profession, and she "discovered" Fleischman's book by reading it after she had read a positive review in a professional journal. Reading reviews is *sometimes* a necessary step for her, but reading (or at least skimming) the book itself is *always* a necessary step. "It's impossible to read every single book that comes in; however, if I don't at least skim them, how do I know the joys they hold? My endorsements are always authentic."

Most teachers are so busy with the everyday "busy-ness" of teaching that they do not have time to read as extensively as the three individuals I have described. Perhaps it is because most teachers think that including fine literature in the reading program will be additional work that otherwise dedicated professionals shrink from the task. Let me assure you that you need not find it overwhelming. There are innumerable resources readily available for classroom teachers who decide to enhance their reading curriculum with the very best books published.

Teachers not only need to read what they recommend, they need to listen to their students, too. Frequently, students are overheard saying, "I just finished reading this great book!" Those are the books teachers probably should read first. We should be taught by our students. Further, children should be given gradual responsibility for using reference books to select their own reading matter.

Those who want the latest Natalie Babbitt or Katherine Paterson books need to know how to locate them.

Here, then, is a comprehensive list of resources for teachers. It consists of bibliographies; indexes; subject encyclopedias; publishers' newsletters, catalogs, guides, and bio sheets; directories; biographical dictionaries/encyclopedias; handbooks; review sources; textbooks and anthologies; booklists; and professional organizations. Depending on teachers' purposes and the needs of their students, referring to only one source at a time will probably suffice in the quest for "real" books.

Bibliographies

Bibliographies, which may be either broad or limited in scope, are alphabetically organized lists of books. In essence, the library's card catalog is a bibliographic inventory organized by title, author, and subject. Teachers find immediate answers from the catalog for books in the library's collection. For books not in the collection of a particular library, a reliable, annual publication, *Children's Books in Print*, is a broad selection guide organized in two volumes: one according to author, title, and illustrator and the other according to subject. There are 6,478 categories in the 1985-1986 subject index and 45,474 children's books listed in its companion volume. Another reference, Carolyn Lima's (1985) *A to Zoo: Subject Access to Children's Picture Books*, lists 4,400 picture books for preschool through second grade, according to 543 subjects. These include ABC books, cumulative tales, and wordless books. John Gillespie's *The Elementary School Paperback Collection* (1985) is equally ambitious in annotating 4,000 paperbacks for young readers, with titles arranged by popular interest.

Among the specific subject bibliographies are *The A.A.A.S. Science Book List for Children* (Deason, 1972) published by the American Association for the Advancement of Science, which lists more than 1,500 science and math books for the elementary grades; *American Historical Fiction and Biography for Children and Young People* (Hotchkiss, 1973), which annotates 1,600 titles arranged both chronologically and by topic; *Books on American Indians and Eskimos* (Lass-Woodfin, 1978), which critically annotates 804 fiction and nonfiction titles and suggests possible uses; *African-Asian Reading Guide for Children and Young Adults* (Hotchkiss, 1976), which lists 1,200 titles concerned with the past and present in Africa, Asia, Australia, and the South Seas; *More Notes from a Different Drummer* and *Books for the Gifted Child* (Baskin & Harris, 1984), which consider books about the handicapped and the gifted, respectively; and *Books in Spanish for Children and Young Adults* (Schon, 1985), which annotates titles about the lifestyle, folklore, heroes, and history of Hispanic cultures. *Children's Books of International Interest* (Elleman, 1985) annotates more than 350 books that either "incorporate universal themes or depict the American way of life." *Juvenile Judaica: The Jewish Values Bookfinder* (Posner, 1985) annotates popular fiction and nonfiction.

Indexes

Although in a broad sense the card catalog is an index to a library's holdings, there are indexes to help teachers locate more finite information about books. For example, *Index to Fairy Tales* (Ireland, 1979) is a valuable source for locating specific tales in collections. It is arranged by title and subject and analyzes 130 collections. *Index to Poetry for Children and Young People* (Brewton et al., 1983), which is part of a multivolume reference series, lists thousands of poems according to title, subject, author, and first lines. *Index to Collective Biographies for Young Readers* (Silverman, 1979) indexes more than 7,000 people representing the contents of close to 1,000 collective biographies. *Children's Book Review Index* (Tarbert, 1975) tells teachers where to locate specific book reviews which have appeared in more than 300 periodicals. The reviews themselves are not provided, however. Teachers will have a field day and get lost for hours in these indexes.

Subject Encyclopedias

The scope of subject encyclopedias is limited to an in-depth consideration of a particular topic. They are good for background information. Within each volume, there is an alphabetical arrangement, and a new volume is sometimes published annually. *Encyclopedia of Fairies: Hobgoblins, Brownies, Bogies, and Other Supernatural Creatures* (Briggs, 1978), is filled with interesting material such as how to distinguish between good and evil fairies.

Publishers' Newsletters, Catalogs, Guides, and Bio Sheets

Publishers will send teachers newsletters and other promotional materials about their books, just for the asking. Teachers should write to the publishers–addresses are easily obtained from the reference librarian or the back of a textbook such as *Literature and the Child* (Cullinan, Karrer, & Pillar, 1981)—to request that their names be added to the mailing list. Newsletters often include interviews with authors, lists of books that have received awards, descriptions of free materials such as posters and bookmarks, and annotations for new books. They also give information about media tie-ins.

Frequently, catalogs will include interesting biographical data about authors and illustrators, in addition to listing books, prices, and ordering information. The 1986 *Viking Penguin Children's Books* catalog, for example, has notes for teachers called "Focus on a Subject" and "Focus on an Author" to help plan units of study. There is even a game, "Do You Know...Who's Who?" on the inside back cover.

Directories

Directories provide systematic lists of people and organizations. Although it will not help teachers with book selection, *Guest Author: A Directory of Speakers* (Manthorne & Moorachian, 1978) is valuable insofar as it lists people involved with books and the subjects they will speak about if invited to a school. It is arranged alphabetically and gives the remuneration the speakers expect.

Children's Books: Awards and Prizes (1985) from The Children's Book Council is probably the most comprehensive compilation available; it catalogs major United States, British Commonwealth, and international book awards. Each entry includes a brief description of the award and a chronological list of winning titles.

Biographical Dictionaries/Encyclopedias

These self-contained volumes, with information about individuals, may cover all periods of time and all countries, or may be limited in scope. *Illustrators of Children's Books* (Kingman et al., 1978) includes critical essays for current entries and updated information on previous volumes. *Something About the Author* (Commire, 1985) is appropriate reading for students and teachers. Including early figures such as John Newbery and L. Frank Baum, the series gives a thorough account of each life in sections entitled Personal, Career, and Writing. If the author's work has been "reworked" in another medium, this information is in "Adaptations." "For More Information" presents other books, reviews, and articles in which the person appears. But most interesting of all is "Sidelights," which contains direct remarks from the authors themselves. Graphics, portraits, and illustrations make this series very appealing. The information will help teachers set an author's work in perspective.

Handbooks

In general, handbooks provide miscellaneous facts related to a specific topic. Their strength is that they present considerable information on a single subject. The most popular one for teachers today is Jim Trelease's (1985) *The Read-Aloud Handbook*. The author tells parents and teachers how to get children to want to read and how to turn them into book lovers. *For Reading Out Loud!: A Guide to Sharing Books with Children* by Margaret Mary Kimmel and Elizabeth Segel (1983) and *Choosing Books for Children: A Commonsense Guide* by Betsy Hearne (1981) are two other fine guides for tracking down good books and for sharing them with children.

Rudine Sims's (1982) in *Shadow and Substance: Afro-American Experience in Contemporary Children's Fiction* surveys 150 books for preschool through grade eight. In a chapter entitled "The Image Makers," the author profiles major Afro-American writers. This valuable book helps teachers and librarians make informed decisions regarding recent literature. Another reference, *Her Way: A Guide to Biographies of Women for Young People,* edited by Mary-Ellen Siegel (1984), is a rich resource of biographies of 1,100 historical and contemporary women. The books included are free of race and sex bias. *Talking About Books* is a curriculum handbook developed by the Parkway School District in Chesterfield, Missouri. The manual for grades K-1 includes lessons, with discussion questions and related creative activities, for *Anno's Journey, Corduroy, On Market Street,* and *The Very Hungry Caterpillar.*

Review Sources

Among the many review sources available to teachers are *Booklist* (American Library Association), *Bulletin of the Center for Children's Books* (University of Chicago Graduate Library School), *The Horn Book Magazine,* (Horn Book), *Publishers Weekly* and *School Library Journal* (Bowker), *Top of the News* (American Library Association), and *The Web* (Ohio State University). Teachers will have to look at each of these sources firsthand to determine the extent of their usefulness. *Booklist,* for example, is quite comprehensive and includes media evaluations. *Popular Reading for Children II: A Collection of Booklist Columns* is an important aid for identifying topics of interest to students in grades two to nine. In contrast, *The Web* is thematically or-

ganized and includes excellent teaching ideas. Each issue contains a comprehensive web of related books and activities.

Textbooks and Anthologies

Each year there is a new text about children's literature. My personal favorite is *Literature and the Child* (Cullinan, Karrer, & Pillar, 1981). It is filled with teaching ideas and activities for using books in the elementary classroom and with curriculum units (primary, intermediate, advanced) such as "My Body and How It Works," "Using the World's Resources in a More Resourceful Way," and "Endangered Species." Two additional favorites are Charlotte Huck, Susan Hepler, and Janet Hickman's *Children's Literature in the Elementary School* (1987) and Zena Sutherland and May Hill Arbuthnot's *Children and Books* (1986).

The two volumes of *The World Treasury of Children's Literature* selected by Clifton Fadiman should be on every teacher's desk and in every parent's library. The volumes contain poems, stories, and extracts from novels–the best of the old and the new–to delight adults and children. Fadiman's essay "For Grown-Ups Only" is essential reading.

It is heartening to see the many poetry collections on the market. In addition to the longtime favorites *Where the Sidewalk Ends* by Shel Silverstein and *One At a Time* by David McCord, here are some other outstanding books with poems: *The Oxford Book of Children's Verse in America* chosen and edited by Donald Hall; *The Random House Book of Poetry for Children* and *The New Kid on the Block* by Jack Prelutsky; *Poems of Lewis Carroll* selected by Myra Cohn Livingston; and *Poetspeak: In Their Work, About*

Their Work by Paul Janeczko. The Janeczko title is for more mature readers.

Nancy Larrick has contributed some notable anthologies for parents and teachers to use. Among them are *On City Streets, Piping Down the Valleys Wild,* and *When the Dark Comes Dancing.*

Lee Bennett Hopkins, anthologist and poet, has credits too numerous to list. However, teachers should know that many of his collections center on special themes: *Munching* dishes up delectables about eating; *Best Friends* discusses friendship; and *The Sea Is Calling Me* concerns sandpiles, lighthouses, and seagulls (what you see at the sea!). Hopkins's *Pass the Poetry, Please! The Revised Edition* (1987) presents in-depth interviews and biographical sketches of America's leading poets for children from A (Arnold Adoff) to S (Shel Silverstein). This indispensable guide offers many activities for delighting children through poetry.

Booklists

Booklists are just that: lists of books either collected on a specific topic or organized according to a given award. These lists may or may not be annotated. Some of them may resemble the bibliographies described earlier, but are not always as comprehensive.

Numerous lists appear in *Booklist,* including "Children's Editors' Choice" and "Notable Children's Books." The Children's Book Council produces booklists with the following organizations: National Science Teachers Association, "Outstanding Science Trade Books for Children"; National Council for the Social Studies, "Notable Children's Trade Books in the Field of Social Studies"; and International Reading Association, "Children's Choices."

Nancy Roser and Margaret Frith's (1983) *Children's Choices: Teaching with Books Children Like* has many suggestions for effective classroom use of children's favorite books.

Dianne Monson (1985), with the National Council of Teachers of English Elementary Booklist Committee, edited *Adventuring with Books: A Booklist for Pre-K to Grade 6.* It lists almost 1,700 children's books published between 1981 and 1984. Monson's expertise shines through in this selection of books with literary and artistic quality. NCTE also publishes "Teachers' Choices," an annual list of books selected by teachers for their literary quality and curriculum uses. Another booklist for teachers is *The Black Experience in Children's Books* by Barbara Rollock (1984), which has almost 800 stories for children from preschool to grade six.

Professional Organizations

There are many benefits for teachers who join professional organizations. Most important are the opportunities membership provides for keeping informed about current practices and policies. Often, these organizations publish extensively on all aspects of teaching and research, including children's literature. The groups listed will send membership information on request.

American Library Association
50 E. Huron Street
Chicago, Illinois 60611

International Reading Association
800 Barksdale Road
P.O. Box 8139
Newark, Delaware 19714-8139

National Council of Teachers of English
1111 Kenyon Road
Urbana, Illinois 61801
(The Children's Literature Assembly (CLA) and the Assembly on Literature for Adolescents (ALAN) are groups within NCTE.)

United States Board on Books for Young People (USBBY)
National Section of the International Board on Books for Young People (IBBY)
c/o International Reading Association
800 Barksdale Road
P.O. Box 8139
Newark, Delaware 19714-8139

Children's Literature Association
210 Education Building
Purdue University
West Lafayette, Indiana 47907

The Children's Book Council
67 Irving Place
New York, New York 10003
(Although individuals cannot join the Council, there is a one time fee that will place you on the mailing list to receive *CBC Features* and other valuable information about children's books and their creators.)

Conclusion

At first glance, the resources described here may appear overwhelming: There are so many of them. For teachers who want to include children's books in the reading program, a logical place to start should be based upon the students' needs. If we know our students' interests, concerns, and world, the first step will be easy.

Each resource will take us to a book. We need to read those books, buy them, and begin to build a classroom collection. We should listen to what our students have to say about books we may never get to read for ourselves. We must ask students, "Have you read any good books lately?" The responses will teach *us*. Most of all, as we step lively toward making fine children's literature part of our reading program, we would do well to remember Emily Dickinson's lines, "There is no frigate like a book/To take us lands away...."

References

Baskin, Barbara, and Harris, Karen. *More notes from a different drummer: A guide to juvenile fiction portraying the disabled*. New York: Bowker, 1984.

Baskin, Barbara, and Harris, Karen. *Books for the gifted child*. New York: Bowker, 1980.

Brewton, John E. et al. (Compilers). *Index to poetry for children and young people: 1976-1981*. New York: Wilson, 1983.

Briggs, Katharine M. *Encyclopedia of fairies: Hobgoblins, brownies, bogies, and other supernatural creatures*. New York: Pantheon, 1978.

Children's books in print. New York: Bowker, 1969--.

Children's books: Awards and prizes. New York: The Children's Book Council, 1986.

Commire, Anne (Ed.). *Something about the author: Facts and pictures about contemporary authors and illustrators of books for young people*. Volumes 1-40. Detroit: Gale, 1985.

Cullinan, Bernice E., Karrer, Mary K., and Pillar, Arlene M. *Literature and the child*. New York: Harcourt Brace Jovanovich, 1981.

Deason, Hilary J. (Compiler). *The A.A.A.S. science book list for children*, third edition. Washington: American Association for the Advancement of Science, 1972.

Elleman, Barbara (Ed.). *Children's books of international interest*, third edition. Chicago: American Library Association, 1985.

Gillespie, John. *The elementary school paperback collection*. Chicago: American Library Association, 1985.

Hall, Donald (Ed.). *The Oxford book of children's books in America*. New York: Oxford University Press, 1985.

Hearne, Betsy. *Choosing books for children: A commonsense guide*. New York: Delacorte, 1981.

Hopkins, Lee Bennett. *Pass the poetry, please!, The Revised Edition*. New York: Harper & Row, 1987.

Hotchkiss, Jeanette Kennan. *African-Asian reading guide for children and young adults*. Metuchen, NJ: Scarecrow Press, 1976.

Hotchkiss, Jeanette Kennan. *American historical fiction and biography for children and young people*. Metuchen, NJ: Scarecrow Press, 1973.

Huck, Charlotte S., Hepler, Susan, and Hickman, Janet. *Children's literature in the elementary school*, fourth revision. New York: Holt, Rinehart and Winston, 1987.

Ireland, Norma O. *Index to fairy tales, 1973-1977: Including folklore, legends, and myths in collections*. Metuchen, NJ: Scarecrow Press, 1979.

Janeczko, Paul B. (Selector). *Poetspeak: In their work, about their work*. New York: Bradbury, 1983.

Kimmel, Margaret Mary, and Segel, Elizabeth. *For reading out loud! A guide to sharing books with children*. New York: Delacorte, 1983.

Kingman, Lee et al. (Eds.). *Illustrators of children's books: 1967-1976*, volume 4. Boston: The Horn Book, 1978.

Lass-Woodfin, Mary Jo (Ed.). *Books on American Indians and Eskimos: A selection guide for children and young adults*. Chicago: American Library Association, 1978.

Lima, Carolyn W. *A to zoo: Subject access to children's picture books*, second edition. New York: Bowker, 1985.

Manthorne, Jane, and Moorachian, Rose (Compilers). *Guest author: A directory of speakers*. Brockton, MA: Hermes, 1978.

Monson, Dianne (Ed.). *Adventuring with books: A booklist for pre-K to grade 6*. Urbana, IL: National Council of Teachers of English, 1985.

Posner, Marcia W. (Ed.). *Juvenile Judaica: The Jewish values bookfinder, an annotated English language bibliography*. New York: Association of Jewish Libraries, 1985.

Rollock, Barbara. *The black experience in children's books*. New York: New York Public Library, 1984.

Roser, Nancy, and Frith, Margaret (Eds.). *Children's choices: Teaching with books children like*. Newark, DE: International Reading Association, 1983.

Schon, Isabel. *Books in Spanish for children and young adults: An annotated guide*. Metuchen, NJ: Scarecrow Press, 1985.

Siegel, Mary-Ellen (Ed.). *Her way: A guide to biographies of women for young people*, second edition. Chicago: American Library Association, 1984.

Silverman, Judith (Ed.). *Index to collective biographies for young readers*, third edition. New York: Bowker, 1979.

Sims, Rudine. *Shadow and substance: Afro-American experience in contemporary children's fiction*. Urbana, IL: National Council of Teachers of English, 1982.

Sutherland, Zena, and Arbuthnot, May Hill. *Children and books*. Chicago: Scott, Foresman, 1986.

Talking about books. Chesterfield, MO: Parkway School District, n.d.

Tarbert, Gary C. (Ed.). *Children's book review index*. Detroit: Gale, 1975--.

Trelease, Jim. *The Read-Aloud Handbook*, second edition. New York: Penguin, 1985.

Children's Books

Fadiman, Clifton. *The World Treasury of Children's Literature*. Little, Brown, 1985.

Fleischman, Paul. *Coming-and-Going Men*. Harper & Row, 1985.

Fritz, Jean. *Make Way for Sam Houston*. G.P. Putnam's Sons, 1986.

Hewitt, Kathryn. *The Three Sillies*. Harcourt Brace Jovanovich, 1986.

Hopkins, Lee Bennett (Selector). *Best Friends*. Harper & Row, 1986.

Hopkins, Lee Bennett (Selector). *Munching: Poems about Eating*. Little, Brown, 1985.

Hopkins, Lee Bennett (Selector). *The Sea Is Calling Me*. Harcourt Brace Jovanovich, 1986.

Larrick, Nancy (Ed.). *On City Streets*. M. Evans, 1968.

Larrick, Nancy (Ed.). *Piping Down the Valleys Wild*. Dell, 1968.

Larrick, Nancy (Ed.). *When the Dark Comes Dancing: A Bedtime Poetry Book*. Philomel, 1983.

Livingston, Myra Cohn (Selector). *The Poems of Lewis Carroll*. Crowell, 1973.

McCord, David. *One at a Time*. Little, Brown, 1977.

Prelutsky, Jack. *The New Kid on the Block*. Greenwillow, 1984.

Prelutsky, Jack. *The Random House Book of Poetry for Children*. Illustrated by Arnold Lobel. Random House, 1983.

Rockwell, Anne. *The Three Sillies and 10 Other Stories to Read Aloud*. Harper & Row, 1986.

Silverstein, Shel. *Where the Sidewalk Ends*. Harper & Row, 1974.

Index of Children's Authors

Index of Children's Books